THE DREAM WORKBOOK

Discover the Knowledge and Power Hidden in Your Dreams

Jill Morris, PH. D.

FAWCETT CREST • NEW YORK

A Fawcett Crest Book
Published by Ballantine Books
Copyright © 1985 by Jill Morris, Ph.D.

Library of Congress Catalog Card Number: 84-28897

ISBN 0-449-21041-3

This edition reprinted by arrangement with Little Brown and Company, Inc.

The excerpt from *Brain/Mind Bulletin* is reproduced by permission
of Interface Press, Box 42211, Los Angeles, California 90042.

Manufactured in the United States of America

First Ballantine Books Edition: February 1987

TAKE AN ENJOYABLE, PROVOCATIVE, VALUABLE JOURNEY INTO THE WORLD OF YOUR DREAMS.

"A clear and sympathetic book exploring and explaining new approaches to dream and fantasy work—the life of our inner selves. A rewarding experience."

Leon Edel, author of
Stuff of Sleep and Dreams: Experiments in Literary Psychology

"Working with our dreams is the safest, most direct way to gain access to the creative depths of our unconscious. In her book, Dr. Morris enables her readers to make the voyage in several different ways—all of them enjoyable, provocative, and valuable. THE DREAM WORKBOOK is an excellent guide for the exploration of one's inner life."

Stanley Krippner, Ph.D.
Faculty Chairman of Saybrook Institute
Author of *Human Possibilities: Mind Research in the U.S.S.R.*

"Jill Morris has presented a fine, organized, and integrated view of dreams from all available perspectives. She makes it possible to use one's dreams for self-realization. She convinces us that working with our dreams is a life-enriching experience."

Hyman Spotnitz, M.D., Med. Sc.D.
Honorary President of the Manhattan Center for Advanced Psychoanalytic Studies
Author of *Modern Psychoanalysis of the Schizophrenic Patient*

Acknowledgment

I want to give special thanks and credit to Gina Rubinstein for her nonstop encouragement right from the beginning, her invaluable and exhaustive help in researching and editing this book, her writing of the "Decoding Your Nightmares" chapter, and her many gifts of dreams and dreamwork. Not only has she been an inspiration to me, but she is an exceptionally talented screenwriter and playwright.

Contents

Introduction

*S*ince ancient times, people have been tantalized and tormented by their dreams. Where do those fleeting, mysterious images come from? What do they mean? How do they affect our waking lives? Man's attempt to answer these questions has given birth to a wide variety of exercises known as dreamwork. Though they differ in their perspectives and goals, this common thread runs through them all: dreamwork is an unfailing catalyst for self-discovery. It's virtually impossible to work with a dream, your own or someone else's, and not obtain some kind of revelation or insight. This innate potential, present in a single dream, is multiplied by the amount of time spent dreaming. We are asleep during approximately one-third of our lives, and we are dreaming fifteen to twenty-five percent of that time.[1] It doesn't require a lot of complicated mathematics to recognize that dreams consume a large portion of our lives, and yet most of us ignore them. Almost as much time is occupied by dreaming as it is by eating; compare all the attention given to the consumption of food and you begin to see how relatively neglected this vast storehouse of insight is.

Dreams are perhaps the ultimate personal creation; for most of us they come from a part so deep within that even we, our conscious selves, have little control over them. But dreams are also the door, the flying carpet if you will, that can lead us to the untapped truths and possibilities that lie within us. For centuries, prophets and sages have consulted dreams to gain mastery over life. Freud considered dreams the most important source of information concerning our unconscious processes. And Henry David Thoreau certainly acknowledged the wisdom contained in dreams when he wrote, "In dreams, we never deceive ourselves, nor are deceived.... In dreams we act a part which we must have learned and rehearsed in our waking hours.... Our truest life is when we are in dreams awake."[2]

But some people fear their dreams as a kind of Pandora's box, comprised of evil wishes and thoughts, that is best left unopened. Theirs is the age-old adage: "What you don't know can't hurt you." They dread reexperiencing past hurts and humiliations and want to avoid sudden glimpses of themselves that fall below their idealized self-image. Their fear, however, is self-defeating because it blocks the self-discovery that could assuage these pains. By examining your dreams rather than avoiding them, crucial concealed knowledge will be revealed and you can begin to understand how the hidden facts of your personality affect your waking life. With more intensive dreamwork, you can easily learn to use this knowledge to help solve problems, overcome fears, enhance creativity, and increase your ability to get the most out of life. Understanding your dreams can awaken you to your inner guide.

How to use this book

The goal of this book is to enable you to remember your dreams, understand them, and become actively involved with them in order to extract their maximum value. Gaining access to your inherent power isn't difficult. The exercises are designed so that the pertinent information effortlessly rises to the surface, seemingly of its own accord. You will find here the psychological and scientific theories that serve as a foundation for understanding the intentions of the different exercises, but one theory is not promoted over another. This is not so much a theoretical treatise as a hands-on workbook.

Dreaming is a function of the right hemisphere of the brain, our creative, emotional side that is too often neglected in a culture that favors the logical linear traits of the left side of the brain. Stimulating the right brain's performance through dreamwork, no matter what the theoretical bias, helps us to bring these two parts of ourselves into harmony, giving us a richer, more complete experience of life.

There is a wide variety of exercises in this book, some to be done alone and others with a dream partner. Certain exercises, like keeping a symbol dictionary and amplifying or expanding a key dream image, are designed to help you discover the meaning of your dreams. Other exercises—such as resolving dreams through rewriting their endings or the Senoi aborigines' approaches to conquering fear and obtaining pleasure in dreams—are geared to enabling you to use your dreams to free yourself from repetitious, counterproductive patterns of thought and behavior. It's important to take all your dreams seriously, and to work with dreams from your childhood and recent past as well as current ones. This is a personal voyage and your dream journal is your diary. And remember, *dreamwork is fun*; enjoy the treasure hunt! Even a nightmare can contain a hidden, positive message. Think of this book as a painter's palette; it provides all the necessary colors but needs you, the artist, to transform them into a work of art.

What can you expect from doing these exercises? It depends on what you want. If you're an artist or writer looking to increase your creativity you'll have different results from those you'd get trying to understand a recurring nightmare or solve a personal problem. Every time you work with a dream the outcome may be different, just as every dream, dreamwork exercise, and moment of your life is different. The one thing you can count on is surprise. Dreamwork, when done assiduously, never provides predictable answers. Sometimes there will be immediate resolutions; other times the answers will come in bits and pieces from several dreams, fragments that will ultimately form a whole. And if one exercise does not provide the results you want, try another. You don't have to follow the sequence of exercises in the book. You may use only a few, or try them all. By experimenting with the exercises, however, you can discover the ones that work for you. The aim of this book is to offer you the widest selection of choices. There are no miracles or guarantees but this—the more you work with your dreams and incorporate your dream experiences into your waking life, the more you will discover all that you are. And the valuable potential within you, waiting to be expressed, is limitless.

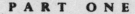

PART ONE

*How to Make
the Most of
Your Dreams*

1

The Science of Sleep and Dreams

*S*ince the beginning of time, people have sought to understand and use their dreams. At the end of the sixth century B.C. people went to Greek temples and slept among huge snakes, believed to be the symbolic carriers of healing, in order to obtain a curative dream from a god.[1] In the Old Testament, God's Will made itself known through the dreams and visions of prophets. By the second century A.D., a wide variety of dream theories prevailed, from the mystical to the medical to the analytical. It was only in the eighteenth and nineteenth centuries, with the rise of the natural sciences, that dreams lost their prestige. Most Eastern and tribal cultures, however, never lost sight of their importance. One of Freud's major contributions was to reawaken the Western world to the value of dreams. When he set out to prove the significance of dreams at the turn of the century, his ideas were still mere theories. Not until the 1950s, when researchers all over the world observed hundreds of thousands of sleeping people, was there any scientific data on dreaming. With the discovery of REM (rapid eye movement) dreaming in 1953, researchers learned how crucial dreams are to our mental health. It was finally proven that all people dream, whether or not they remember doing so.

The nature of sleep

Eugene Aserinsky, observing sleeping babies during an experiment at the University of Chicago, noticed that at certain times during sleep the babies' eyes moved back and forth under their closed eyelids.[2] Further experiments were conducted in which adult subjects were awakened during these periods of rapid eye movement. Eighty percent of these subjects reported being eng. ed in vivid dreams. Dreamers' eyes move back and forth as if they are watching an event; this is not surprising, since dreams are primarily visual. It's as if all our thoughts, feelings, and sensations are translated into mental pictures. As might be expected, the dreams of blind people, especially those blind from birth, are somewhat different. Instead of visual images, the dream consists of experiences of the other senses, such as hearing, touch, and smell. In those not blind from birth, the dreams eventually lose their visual qualities and are composed of only the other senses.[3]

Dreams were once thought to be exclusive to the REM state, but researchers later discovered that dreaming also takes place during other phases of sleep.[4]

Dreams arising during non-REM sleep are shorter and less visual and vivid than their REM counterparts. Usually concerned with current problems, they often involve logical reasoning and don't seem like dreams at all; many people experience them as periods of being awake and "just thinking."[5] Dreams also occur during the hypnogogic state—that transitory period between wakefulness and sleep. These dreams usually involve strange body sensations, surrealistic conversations, and hallucinations. They are similar to REM dreams in nature but are shorter and don't involve rapid eye movement.[6] All dreams can be revealing, but REM dreams are the most vivid and expressive.

As some of you may have experienced, the depth of your sleep is not consistent throughout the night. Researchers have determined that there are four separate stages of sleep, with much movement between them during the course of the night. Sleep begins with the drifting sensations of Descending Stage One and gets progressively deeper (with accompanying brain-wave changes) in Stages Two and Three until Stage Four, where the brain's electrical rhythm is slow, with high-voltage waves.[7] At this point the muscles of your body are totally relaxed and you rarely move.[8] When you've reached Stage Four you then return through Stages Three and Two to Emergent Stage One,[9] where most of your dreaming occurs. This cycle through the sleep stages takes approximately ninety minutes and recurs about every ninety minutes thereafter, with four to seven repetitions a night.[10] Each period of dreaming is longer than the one preceding it; the initial dream state may last five to ten minutes, while the final one can be forty minutes long.[11] Nightmares, which can seem to go on for-

ever, usually run only twenty minutes.[12] Fifteen to
twenty-five percent of an average night's sleep is spent
dreaming, with the longest periods occurring in the early
morning hours. It's during the final hour that you're
likely to have your most significant dreams. This timing
is propitious since the dreams you have just before waking are the easiest to recall.

Sleep, and consequently dreaming, is not the passive
state that you might assume; indeed, it is often anything
but tranquil. Scientists today no longer define sleep as
the absence of activity but rather as a different kind of
activity. They've discovered there's an entire set of
nerve cells that *actively* inhibit the waking state and
cause sleep.[13] During dreams, our physiological activities
(including heart rate, blood pressure, respiration, and
sporadic activity of certain fine muscle groups) increase
from the customary sleeping levels to a state similar to
wakefulness.[14] Cerebral blood flow accelerates, the met-
abolic rate increases, and sometimes brain temperature
rises as well. During peak REM times the heart and res-
piratory functions can fluctuate wildly. This may, in part,
account for the heart attacks that sometimes occur during sleep.[15] In contrast, there is a decrease in muscle tone
when we dream. It has been suggested that this is the
body's way of protecting itself against actually performing the actions being experienced in the dream.[16] Freud
believed we could have intense experiences and taboo
feelings in our dreams because it was physically impossible to act them out. The nerve cells that govern motivation and memory turn off during REM dreaming, which
is why most dreams are involuntary and amnesiac.[17] Of
course, turbulent activity is not usually the primary sensation during sleep. If you're one of the many who enjoy

sleeping late on the weekends, you'll be interested to know that there's probably a physical basis behind it. Part of the sleep pathway passes through the newly discovered, and much discussed pleasure center of the brain.[18] This could explain the luxuriously sensuous and satisfying feeling of sleep.

Recent dream discoveries

Recent experiments in France suggest that genetics plays a role in dreaming. Michael Jouvet, Europe's leading theoretician on sleep, has done research on identical twins (those with the same genetic components) that shows an unusual similarity in their REM patterns, far greater than those between "regular" brothers and sisters. He found that they shared the same timing and duration of REM periods.[19] While acknowledging that the brain is far too complicated a mechanism to be solely genetically determined, and that other factors such as environment play a large role, he explains these similarities by theorizing that the part of the brain that controls the dream state is governed by heredity.[20] While Jouvet's study didn't compare the actual dreams of twins, he notes there were a couple of instances where twins had the same dreams.

A patient who has never considered herself close to her identical twin sister has also mentioned several occasions when she and her sister had the same dream on the same night. Jouvet's study of twins' dreams may have raised more questions than it answered, but it certainly points to an interesting new area of dream research.

Research has been done in Russia that appears to

substantiate the ancient belief in the use of dreams as an adjunct to medicine. Scientists there report being able to predict the beginnings of physical illnesses from their patients' dreams. These diseases were not discovered through conventional medical tests, and as a result of the dreams, and their interpretations, many lives were saved.[21]

Whether or not we recall or use our dreams, it's essential to our well-being that we have them. When we don't dream, we become anxious, irritable, and have difficulty concentrating. Prolonged REM deprivation can lead to intense hunger accompanied by feelings of emptiness and depression. In some instances there are psychotic symptoms and hallucinations.[22] One of the dangers of alcohol is that it has been proven to cut dreaming time short.[23] When an alcoholic withdraws from the addiction, almost one hundred percent of his or her sleep time is spent dreaming.[24] This is because a person deprived of dreaming time recovers REM sleep on subsequent nights in almost the exact amount of the previous deprivation. However, when a person is deprived of nondreaming time, there is no need to make up for the lost sleep.[25] It appears that our bodies may know something about the importance of dreams that our minds are only beginning to comprehend now.

Age and gender

Interesting and controversial information has surfaced about the roles of age and gender in dreams. Newborn infants spend about fifty percent of their sleep time in the REM state; in premature babies that percentage can rise as high as seventy-five percent. By age five the percentage of REM time is twenty-five to thirty percent, and in adolescence the rate drops to twenty percent. Dream time remains at that level until about age sixty, when the REM rate is lowered to fifteen percent.[26] Infants obviously can't report the content of their dreams, but we do know that small children's dreams may be markedly different from those of adults. The majority of small children's dreams contain animals, especially lions, tigers, spiders, wolves, gorillas, and alligators. As children grow older the percentage of animal characters decreases; by the time they reach adulthood they will dream of animals less than eight percent of the time.[27] Children usually see themselves as victims of others in their dreams, and their most frequent dream emotions are fear and apprehension. Clearly they too express waking life tensions in their dreams.[28] Perhaps this is one reason why some children find bedtime a traumatic occasion.

Gender differences in dreams appear during childhood. Boys mention more tools and other objects in their dreams, while girls have longer dreams with more people in them. In adults, men seem to have more sexual, physically active, and aggressive dreams, while women emphasize the emotions and conversations in their dreams and are more often the victims of others' aggression.[29] Although these generalizations are theoretically interesting, many dreams contradict these premises. I find it more valuable to examine dreams as individual, unique experiences, without gender and age distinctions.

Right brain, left brain

For the most part, Western culture had accorded dreamers and their dreams little importance, with the current exception of dreams brought to the psychotherapist as an aid to understanding the patient's psyche. This neglect is gradually changing as scientists from fields as diverse as neurophysiology and quantum physics begin to recognize the scientific truth contained in psychic and spiritual phenomena.[30] These processes, it appears, stem largely from right brain activity. Through work on thousands of brain-damaged people and those with neurosurgically separated hemispheres, researchers have discovered that there is an intriguing difference in the alpha wave generation of the right and left hemispheres of the normal brain,[31] with further data indicating that the two halves specialize in different ways of thinking.[32] Robert Evans Ornstein, research psychologist at Langley Porter Neuropsychiatric Institute in San Francisco, and his colleagues have discovered that the left hemisphere specializes in activities that are verbal, logical, numerical, linear, and scientific. The right brain deals with the spatial, artistic, nonlinear, intuitive, creative, emotional, and even perhaps the religious.[33] I would add dreaming to the list of right brain functions since dreams are primarily visual, preverbal, nonrational or based largely on associative thinking, and do not use logical sequences of time and space.

Until recently, we have tended to undermine the right brain to enhance the left. We are now learning that this is neither necessary nor wise. Scientists now agree that the "complete person," able to tap his full potential, is the individual who uses both the left and right hemispheres of his brain—both his rational and intuitive abilities.[34] I am convinced that we must pay attention to our dreams if we are to attain our optimum balance in life and utilize all we have within us. They can provide access to the vital personal truths that our rational minds are unable to fathom.

2

Diary of Discovery:
The Dream Journal

A *dream journal is a diary of one's inner*
journey, a record of one's progress in problem-solving
and an indicator of areas where difficulties still exist. I
use mine as an encyclopedia of my innermost being. It is
my book of wisdom, an intimate part of my existence.

Understanding a single dream is never enough, because it shows only a fragment of the picture. C. G. Jung
never entirely trusted the interpretation of an isolated
dream. He believed certainty of interpretation could be
achieved only by analyzing a series of dreams over an
extended period of time, perhaps years. Only in this way
could he see the fundamental ideas and themes of the
dreamer's struggle, kaleidoscopically revealed through
different aspects of the same situation. Recording your
dreams in a dream journal will afford you the opportunity to view the many facets of your personality; each
dream entered provides another perspective. In this way,

your dream journal can become your personal book of wisdom.

Keeping a dream journal

The first step in working with your dreams is recording them, creating and developing your dream journal. Dreams are forgotten quickly, usually within ten minutes of awakening,[1] and you'll have substantially better results with all the exercises if you have access to details garnered while the dream is still fresh, rather than having to rely on your memories of the dream hours or days later. Your dream journal, however, is more than a mere adjunct to the exercises; it's a powerful catalyst for insight on its own.

Dream journals have been kept for centuries, and a standard, easy procedure has evolved. All you need is a looseleaf notebook, a pad of looseleaf paper, and a pen that writes without pressure (you can even get one with a tiny flashlight attached for writing in the dark). Put the pen and pad where you can reach them easily, such as on the nightstand next to your bed, so that you can record the dream as soon as you awake from it. You can write in the dark by holding the pad in such a way that you can feel its borders. Then just move your hand and arm across the page as you write. When you reach the right-hand edge of the page, drop your hand down an inch and move it straight back to the left (like a typewriter carriage) and begin again. You should end up with fairly legible lines. You may want to tape-record your dreams, a more direct process, but be aware of two disadvantages: you may mumble your words since you're still in a semisleep state, and later you'll have to make a tran-

scription, which is time-consuming and easily post-
poned. Whether you write or tape the dream, you should
have no trouble going back to sleep.

It's essential that you write down your dream immediately, since important details start evaporating in seconds. Jot down the dream's story, themes, symbols,
emotions, key phrases, etc., as they come to you. Include as many details and nuances as you can, but don't
get bogged down trying to find the exact words to describe a complicated or elusive feeling or mood. Label it
"complex" or "many feelings" and go on, so that you
capture the whole dream. Once you have the basic account you can go back and add to these sections. When
you finish writing the dream's plot, put down your associations and feelings toward it, or any parts of it. Below
are key questions specifically devised to elicit the
dream's important insights. Ideally you should answer
the questions right after recording it, but as long as you
have a good initial narrative you'll be able to do this
later.

E X E R C I S E   1

Answering Key Questions

Key Questions
1. What are your feelings upon awakening? Joy, depression, fear, motivation?
2. What real-life memories or prior dreams does this
   dream remind you of?
3. What is the setting of the dream? Indoors, outdoors,
   or both? Is it someplace familiar?
4. Are there colors in the dream? If so, what are your
   associations to these colors?

5. What were the preceding day's events that might have influenced this dream?
6. What are the loaded symbols and key phrases in your dream, and what are your associations to them?
7. What are the other traits, as personified by the other characters in the dream, that might be parts of yourself that you're disowning?

It's certainly not imperative for you to memorize these questions and to answer them all each time. Your interest and the dream itself will determine how deeply you wish to go and which questions you want to pursue. As long as you record the primary details you'll have enough information to do the exercises; but obviously the more you have to work with, the closer you will come to the dream's meaning.

After you've completed your notes, give the date of your dream and assign it a title, based on the most unusual or charged image; this will make it easy to refer to later. Then put it in your looseleaf notebook; dividers will enable you to section the journal off into monthly segments. As your notebook grows, patterns and themes will emerge and future dreams will add new insights to former ones. Keep all your written dreamwork in your dream journal; what you don't understand now may become clear later. How far you go with your dream journal, what you turn it into, is a personal choice. Many people just jot down the plots of their dreams and their basic associations. Others turn their dream journals into mirrors and maps of inner landscapes by writing poems, drawing pictures, and pasting in photographs that remind them of places and images in the dream.

The following is an example of a full dream journal entry.

In the Basement of Van Cleef & Arpels—4/8/83

I'm at a cocktail party on the beach, standing on a
jetty. There are hundreds of beautifully dressed
people on different levels—fifty people on one
level, fifty on another, etc. The levels look like
squares strung together; they rise up like a stair-
case. The whole party is in a shape, similar to a
cut-up cigarette box, made up of these groups of
people in squares. The ocean rushes into the party,
and there are volcanic eruptions, earthquakes,
fires, and storms. None of the people are fazed by
this and the party continues. I am by myself, an
observer and not a participant in the party. The last
image is of a gorgeous volcanic eruption, huge ex-
plosions of red and purple.

Suddenly I'm in the basement of Van Cleef &
Arpels. It doesn't look at all like Van Cleef and
Arpels but I know that's where I am because the
customer I'm waiting on tells me so. That customer
is my friend Suzanne; she is rich, beautiful, and
successful. The basement of Van Cleef & Arpels
has become a clothing store; I am brand-new there
and am selling shoes to people who are better than
I. I ask Suzanne how Papagallo got into the basement of Van Cleef & Arpels but I don't get an answer. I'm amazed to be working there since I don't
know how I got there, and I'm embarrassed to be
waiting on Suzanne. I'm impressed with the quality
and softness of the leather of the shoes. Suzanne
and the other people in the store are distant and
unfazed, the way they were at the party.

Initial Associations In both places I'm surrounded
by people better than I. At the party I'm an outside
observer; then I'm serving someone who has
everything I want. It's clear I *end up* working in the
garment industry—where I used to work; it's defi-

nitely not a goal I've consciously *worked toward.*
I'm afraid that's where I'll end up, never knowing
what I'm meant to do with my life.

After the dreamer wrote this basic account, she answered the Key Questions.

1. Feelings upon awakening: Frightened that it's my
   destiny to serve people who are better than I; depressed and helpless.
2. Memories/prior dreams: *Memories*—of all the times
   I've run into people when I've been in a vulnerable
   position and they've never been vulnerable or disturbed. *Prior dreams*—other dreams of working in
   the garment industry where I also awoke depressed.
3. Settings/places: *Beach*—the Hamptons or Malibu;
   where all the successful people are. *Basement*—the
   bottom of what represents the height of attainment;
   the worst.
4. Colors: *Red* (from volcanic eruption)—regal; explo-
   sive; powerful; out of my control. *Purple* (from volcanic eruption)—wounded; angry; hurtful.
5. Preceding day's events: Dealing with significant insights about my future direction.
6. Symbols/key phrases: *Van Cleef & Arpels* [A re-
   nowned New York Fifth Avenue jewelry store]—the
   epitome of success, luxury, and attainment; everything I want. *Papagallo* [A chain of fashionable
   clothes/shoes boutiques]—first experience with judging products by their brand. *Garment industry*—failure. *"Brand-new"* (the way I describe myself as a
   saleswoman)—a new, untested brand; not yet having
   status; not knowing whether I will ever achieve the

prestige of a "designer label." *"Ended up"* (how I arrived in the basement)—the opposite of going towards and achieving; inertia; equals failure.
7. Other characters' traits: They are inherently successful, worthwhile, cool, and invulnerable. Suzanne belongs to this elite group. I don't see these traits as possible in myself.

The dreamer found a photograph in a magazine that reminded her of the people at the party. The photograph made her realize that the people were faceless; they had no identities. It sparked in her a feeling of ignorance about what it is in others that enables them to be impenetrable and successful in ways she is not.

She found a Van Cleef & Arpels advertisement that represented all the store meant to her—luxury, possession of valuable objects, being "first"—Number One, the very best. She was struck by the slickness of the picture and realized that the characteristic of unperturbed superficiality also described the people in the dream.

The dreamer discovered a photograph that made her think of Suzanne, and her immediate response to the picture was "I want to be her!" She became aware of how envious she was of Suzanne's success and privileges.

Through simply writing her dream in her dream journal and answering the Key Questions, she became conscious of wanting to be invulnerable and untouchable like the others; at the same time, she felt that if she acted this way (which wasn't intrinsically herself) she'd end up nowhere, a failure. She experienced her jealousy of friends she perceived to be "better" than she. Her dream expressed these messages very clearly. Indeed, she felt they were hammered into her.

EXERCISE 2

Making a Symbol Dictionary

As we've seen, most dreams contain a variety of images and symbols. Many symbols, such as houses and bodies of water, are universal, and I discuss their meanings in the chapter "Images, Symbols, and Metaphors." But all symbols are personal, and it's this subjective aspect of them that is most important. Personal symbols derive their meaning from your individual life experiences. Only you know what they mean, and compiling a dictionary of these images can make translating them easier.

To create a symbol dictionary simply add alphabetized looseleaf dividers to the back of your dream journal. Write at the top of a page each important symbol and action that occurs in your dream, then list whatever associations automatically come to mind. Write the title and date of the dream in which it occurred, its role in the dream, and any other pertinent thoughts. You might also find it useful to include pictures of the symbol, of your own drawings or photographs that convey the feeling of the symbol. You'll discover that many important personal symbols will recur in your dreams; each time they do, add to that page the name, date, and relevant information about the dream. By doing so, you'll have a written record of the evolution of that symbol. New meanings and insights will reveal themselves, and as your self-awareness increases you'll be able to chart the way that symbol changes in relationship to your personal growth.

As an example, here's a dream that occurred the night after the dreamer argued with his mother.

Hornets' Nest — 12/8/82

I have brought something inside, or allowed something to enter, that is a type of hornets' nest. I am not alone; someone else is there with me. An enormous hornet crawls out of the nest, lands on the back of my neck, lodges in, and draws blood. It is slightly painful. I have the feeling it has gone in deep, and that it should be more painful than it is. I don't move. More nests appear. They look like water bombs I made as a kid. The other person there is my mother; she pierces each nest and a blue fluid oozes out.

Initial Associations Something dangerous attacks me, and my mother tries to protect me by destroying the enemy.

The following are the dreamer's entries in his symbol dictionary. He also included pictures that evoked their emotional impact. Pictures for your symbol dictionary need not be literal, by the way. A photograph of something completely different can be equally, if not more, effective at eliciting and representing certain moods and feelings.

Hornets' Nest: Bedlam; danger; buzzing; stinging; place to avoid. "Hornets' Nest" 12/8/82—A hornets' nest unleashes a hornet that attacks me.

Hornet: Lethal; stinging; treacherous. "Hornets' Nest" 12/8/82—An enormous hornet comes out of its nest, lands on the back of my neck, and sucks my blood.

Hornet drawing blood from my neck: Blood sucker; draining my life; I dare not move for fear of more injury; I'm frozen, waiting to be released. "Hornets' Nest" 12/8/82—A hornet lands on my neck and draws blood; I don't move. I'm a victim, trapped by something venomous.

Water Bombs: I made them as a kid; they explode. "Hornets' Nest" 12/8/82—More hornets' nests appear and they look like water bombs. They are filled with a blue fluid.

Mother: Life-giving, loving, protective, breasts filled with milk. "Hornets' Nest" 12/8/82—My mother pierces the hornets' nests.

Blue fluid: Octopus ink; octopus has tentacles that entrap. "Hornets' Nest" 12/8/82—When my mother pierces the hornets' nests a blue fluid oozes out.

As the dreamer wrote about his symbols and chose pictures to express them, he had a sudden revelation. A photograph representing the hornet drawing blood from his neck also reminded him of his mother piercing the nests. Continuing the association, he realized that the image made him think of a baby sucking at its mother's breast. The meaning of the dream became clear—the hornet drawing blood from his neck and his mother piercing the nests were essentially two different aspects of his feelings toward his mother. On the one hand, he experienced his mother as venomous and trapping. At the same time, he envisioned her as protective and life-giving; but that perception also included feelings about his early dependency on her that he found unacceptable. This hidden conflict kept him imprisoned, unable to move. The dream provided an imagistic link which connected his different feelings and brought them out into the open.

The symbols that conveyed this message are his own creations and thus are likely to occur again in new contexts. As he adds future manifestations of the symbols to his dictionary he will gain a multifaceted understanding of how these images express hidden emotions. By including illustrations that evoke the feeling of the symbol in the dream, he will have a powerful visual record of its evolution as well.

Remembering your dreams

Of course, keeping a dream journal and symbol diction-ary can be difficult if you have trouble remembering your dreams. Some people even mistakenly claim they don't have dreams since they don't remember them. Dream research reveals that everyone dreams. And there are techniques that can enhance your ability to remember them.

If you're having difficulty, it may help to understand some of the reasons why we forget our dreams. Some people are afraid to remember because of traumatic dreams from the past. A patient of mine said he had only remembered three dreams in his entire life; all occurred during childhood and early adolescence and involved ter-rifying scenes of abandonment and abuse by his parents. In real life his parents were abusing and abandoning him in subtle and insidious ways. He would lie awake all night, afraid to go to sleep for fear of dreaming. It's not surprising that he stopped remembering them. Through dreamwork he learned precisely why they had been so traumatic, and then gradually regained his ability to re-call dreams.

Many of us, understandably, don't want to see certain facets of ourselves or experience painful and disturbing feelings. But these emotions replay themselves in our unconscious minds whether we examine them or not, as anyone who has awakened depressed and unsettled without knowing why can tell you. By exposing our dreams' covert messages we demystify them and diminish their capacity to hurt.

There are a number of things you can do to help yourself recall dreams. One time-proven way is the incubation method, practiced in temples in ancient Greece by people seeking healing dreams. Just as the ancient Greeks invoked the god of healing for a curative dream, you can tell yourself, "I will remember my dreams when I wake up." The time to do this is during the hypnogogic state, that transitory period between waking and sleeping when your mind is very suggestible. During this state, colors and images often pass before your closed eyes, and you may have dreamlike thoughts and experiences. It's also helpful to set your alarm clock a half hour to an hour earlier. Your most productive dreaming period is in the early morning just before you awaken, and waking yourself early can enable you to catch these important dreams.

If you wake up knowing you just had a dream but it escaped you, go back to the sleeping position you were in when you had the dream. Let's say you have been lying on your back (a particularly good position for dreaming) with your head slightly tilted to one side. Take that position again, close your eyes, and allow yourself to drift back into a dreamlike state. If the dream or a fragment of it doesn't return, recall the feelings and images you had when you first awoke. It's also helpful to run through a list of the important people in your life; one of them might have been in your dream and thus can trigger your memory. If the dream still doesn't come back to you, then make one up while you're in this position. When you're drowsy you're close to the dream state and consequently close to your unconscious mind and deeper creativity. The dream exercises will also be effective with a dream you invent.

If, after all this effort, your dreams continue to elude you, don't despair; just stop trying for a while. Your mind may be resisting the pressure, and you may find that once you give yourself permission *not* to remember your dreams, you may start recalling them. You can also work with other people's dreams; surprisingly enough, their dreams can offer you major insights into yourself.

After a couple of weeks, try the incubation method again; there's a good chance you'll be successful this time around.

3

Images, Symbols, and Metaphors

*I*mages, symbols, and metaphors; this is "such stuff as dreams are made on" (Shakespeare, *The Tempest*). These threads are woven together to form the fabric of our dreams; we must unravel them to expose their meaning and discover our dreams' messages. Through understanding how images, symbols, and metaphors are formed, their importance in our lives and dreams emerges.

Images

Although the boundaries between dream images and dream symbols may overlap at times, distinctions do exist. Images are mental representations of objects or persons not physically present; we create them in our unconscious so that we have an inner mental picture of

33

those things that evoke an emotional response in us. Images begin to be formed at about the seventh or eighth month of an infant's life.[1] The baby, at birth, perceives the world and himself through his five senses—touch, taste, smell, sight, and hearing. Images are those perceptions that eventually become internalized because of their emotional significance to the child. For example, an infant hungry for maternal nurturing usually learns through experience to associate satisfaction of that desire with his mother's breast. Through this connection he forms an image of the breast; when that particular need arises in him, he experiences it as a desire for that specific object. The many images thus formed constitute our inner reality—our dreams, thoughts, fantasies, and ideas. Therefore, the images that appear in our dreams are not accidental or purposeless; they have emotional significance for us. It is this emotional connection that gives our images their meaning.

Although images may be exact representations of outer perceptions (you dream of the exact pair of shoes you perceived in a waking state), they can also be distorted. Images don't necessarily exist in isolation and thus can be affected by their context. Emotions or objects that were present, either temporarily or physically, when the image was initially created often continue to be associated with it and can become an integral part of the image. Also, through a mechanism that Freud called "condensation," one image can consist of several seemingly unrelated characteristics, all of which, when understood, suggest an identical underlying feeling. For example, a woman dreams of a wild horse with human hair. Associating to the image, she recalls the adventure stories about wild horses that she loved as a child, and recognizes the human hair on the dream horse as her own when she was in her early twenties. The combined image conveys the desire for unfettered freedom inherent in both her and the horse. In deciphering the images in our dreams, Freud's technique of free association is invaluable.

As the following example illustrates, no two people— regardless of how close they are—will relate to the same significant image in an identical way. A pair of twins reported that pipes and pipe smoke played frequent, though apparently minor, roles in their dreams. Their father had smoked a pipe, and it was clear that the image was connected to being physically close to him. Closer examination, however, revealed markedly different responses to it. One twin associated pipes with a foul odor, claustrophobia, tears in her eyes, and a need to escape. Her sister liked the smell, perceiving it as cozy, warm, and protectively enveloping, and visualized cloudlike tendrils of smoke suspended in midair. Their associations clearly reflected widely divergent experiences of being with their father. Until they exploded this image, they weren't aware how disparate their feelings were. Though pipes might play only peripheral roles in their actual dreams, they saw that the pipe was indeed a significant image.

Symbols

While an image directly represents the object it pictures, a symbol is an object that stands for something else. Symbols are usually connected to the objects, emotions, or ideas they represent through an unconscious association or relationship, and not through objective or intentional resemblance.

Symbols do not appear only in dreams: conscious and unconscious symbols are also influential in our waking lives. How could society exist without them, since words, numbers, traffic signs, etc., are all symbols! The universal human need, evidenced in all cultures, to set up complex social systems and rituals demonstrates that people vastly prefer to deal with the sharply defined representatives of reality rather than the more amorphous reality itself. A prime example of this is the cultural phenomena attendant on marriage ceremonies. The need to maintain kinship systems and form family units is universal and primary. And yet, in essentially all cultures, it is not sufficient merely to form these units. Rituals, in the form of weddings and other marriage ceremonies, are performed as a way of solidifying, making tangible, this need. Marriage and all its accouterments are thus symbols for this basic human instinct. It's interesting to note that many so-called "primitive" cultures have even more complex marriage rites and kinship systems than we do.

Symbols can be generally categorized into four overlapping groups: universal symbols, cultural symbols, creative symbols, and personal symbols.

Universal symbols

Universal symbols are those rooted to the experience of all humankind and thus common to everyone. Jung considered his archetypes of the collective unconscious to be universal symbols, as did Freud with his sexual symbols. Most theoreticians agree that certain universal symbols appear in our dreams. Listed below are a few of the most common ones with their generally accepted meanings:

Common Universal Symbols

House: Self.

Weather: What one is going through in life. For example, a storm represents turmoil; sunshine represents happiness; the cold represents lack of love.

Water: The emotions, the unconscious, the source of all life. The type of water—whether it's a bay, stream, lake, or ocean—and the movement of the water gives clues as to what is happening in the feelings and the unconscious.

Time of Day: The time of one's life or one's state of being. For example, dusk can represent a state of withdrawal or retiring, or it can symbolize approaching the end of one's life. Dawn can mean youth, awakening, and optimism.

It's imperative to understand, however, that the universal meanings and generalized definitions found in dream symbol "dictionaries" are of minimal value in terms of self-understanding and personal growth. Only through discovering your own translations of symbols, even universal ones, can you effect any real change or insight. The exercises in this book are designed to aid you in that process. Another major limitation inherent in shortcut, "all-purpose" symbol definitions is that they ignore the fact that symbols change meaning according to the context in which they appear and the personal experiences of the dreamer. Erich Fromm illustrates this principle with the symbols FIRE and SUN. In a fireplace, fire suggests warmth and pleasure; in a forest, it conveys terror and destruction. To a person living in a northern climate, the sun can be a source of life. To a resident of the Near East, however, it can be scorching and life-threatening.[2]

Cultural symbols

Cultures with a common language also share many of the same symbols, some of which are consciously chosen, and these can appear in dreams. The color RED is a cultural symbol meaning "stop," "danger," "no," or something of importance. Famous people can also be cultural symbols; Woody Allen, for example, seems to appear in many people's dreams. It's easy to interpret him as the all-too-human neurotic, loaded with insecurities. Those who dream of him may unconsciously believe that they possess similar personality traits. The conscious cultural symbol of the cross or crucifix is a good example of the wide scope of meaning that can be attached to a single object. As the symbol of Christianity, the cross represents both the person and life history of Jesus Christ, a complex set of specific doctrines, the history and evolution of both that ideology and the people who have believed in it, and the role that belief system and those people have played in the world throughout history, in the present day, and projected into the future. All that, and more, is encompassed in a simple, single figure. However, as with universal symbols, you won't gain much insight from cultural symbols in your dreams until you dig past their cultural significance and delve deeper into your own personal, unique experience of them.

Creative symbols

Creative symbols are those consciously formed by artists (and I use that designation in its broadest sense) to portray their inner visions in the most succinct, intense, and emotionally impactful ways. As will be mentioned in the "Creativity" chapter, the artist can, and often does, find these symbols in his dreams. In a sense, they are a hybrid of personal symbols and universal ones: they are chosen by an individual, based on his personal experiences and aesthetic perceptions, to express a unique concept, but their intent is to communicate their meaning in a manner that touches the emotions and sensibilities prevalent in us all. The artist, in that way, has the opposite task of the dreamer: the artist has the message and searches for the symbol to express it, and the dreamer has the symbol and seeks to discover the message.

Personal symbols

Personal symbols are the most significant ones in terms of self-awareness and revelation; they are the ones this book addresses. As I've mentioned, this is the most valuable way to approach all symbols.

Personal symbols are formed in a person's unconscious mind and are individually tailored to reflect that person's composite of life experience and emotion. The unconscious is even better than the artist at creating the most perfect symbol to illustrate a particular inner message. Understanding one's personal symbols is one of

the primary goals of dreamwork, and it doesn't require
outside interpreters or strenuous self-examination. The
exercises in this book are specifically designed so that
the mere act of doing them prompts your symbols to
explain themselves. Many of my students received tremendous and immediate insights the first time they did
these exercises. By experimenting with the different exercises, you'll discover which ones work best for you.

E X E R C I S E 3
Talking with Your Symbol

One simple but illuminating way to uncover a symbol's
meaning is to have a conversation with it, in the form of
a written dialogue in your dream journal. This exercise
affords you the opportunity not only to discover the
symbol's meaning in that particular dream, but also to
question it about the broader context of its history, desires, and view of the future. Write spontaneously, without judging or censoring yourself, and allow yourself to
feel the personality of the symbol as it arises in you.

A student decided to try this exercise with the following dream:

The Bear

I'm walking in New York with an enormous bear
on a collar and leash; I'm taking it somewhere.
There is running water along the curb, and we arrive at a hill. We are confronted by scenes of
death: a duck swallows another duck, and a white
dog carries a stillborn pup in its mouth and drops it
down by the gutter.

I love the bear but it's being very rambunctious, pulling at the leash and playfully nipping my hand. Suddenly I'm back in my childhood house in Cleveland, and I put the bear in the upstairs bathroom. I'm having dinner with my family and I try to tell my father that the bear is upstairs, but my father keeps talking and I can't get a word in.

Then I'm back in New York with the bear. I want it to be safe; I feel someone is after it. I take it to a Catholic all-girls' college and put it in a bathroom. I come back two days later to get the bear, and find a note on the bathroom door saying that they have given the bear to this man who really wanted it, and that no amount of money can induce him to return the bear.

The dreamer had no idea what this dream was about, and decided to have a conversation with the bear. By writing out the following dialogue, she found the bear to be a multidimensional character with a compelling message for her. This example, by the way, is exceptionally articulate; your conversation doesn't have to be as witty for it to reveal your symbol's meaning.

Conversation with the Bear

LILY: Who are you?

BEAR: I'm your desire to be something truly great.

LILY: Can you be more specific?

BEAR: Not unless you are.

LILY: Well, what is this great thing I want to be?

BEAR: How do I know? You never bothered to figure that out. I didn't say I was this grand thing, I said I was your desire to be it. You have to fill in your own blanks. I can't do everything.

LILY: Does your appearance in my dream mean

that what I'm doing with my life now isn't good enough?

BEAR: What's "good enough"? I don't know. Maybe it's good enough. If you want to know if you're satisfied ask yourself, don't ask me. I think it's okay, you could be doing worse, but it's hardly Beethoven's Fifth, if you want to talk about being grand.

LILY: Tell me what this dream is about.

BEAR: Aren't you the lazy one. You'll never be anything great with that attitude.

LILY: You know, you're pretty arrogant and obnoxious.

BEAR: What do you expect? Thinking you've got it in you to be the next Martin Luther King or Mother Teresa is pretty arrogant. And anyone would get obnoxious waiting around for you to actually do it. Need I remind you that neither of us is getting any younger?

LILY: Since, as you pointed out, we don't have all the time in the world, could you please condescend to help me out with this dream?

BEAR: Oh, all right. This is it: You've been carrying me around with you for a long time, without knowing what to do with me. You're a little afraid of me, like I can't be trusted and have to be controlled, which is why you keep me on a collar and leash. I hope you realize how ludicrous that is. I mean, I'm twice as big as you, weigh three times as much, and could pull you from here to New Jersey and back if I wanted to. That's not to mention that I could rip the leash in two, yank it out of your hand, or even bite your head off if it struck my fancy. You think you're controlling me because I let you.

LILY: Why don't you take control?

BEAR: Because it's your life. Speaking of which, the death stuff, with the duck and the dog, is a warning that the two of us are not going to be able to pal around forever; at some point it's going to be either you or me.

LILY: Why?

BEAR: I'll get to that later. Now about this habit of yours of sticking me in bathrooms, that's pretty insulting, you know. Acting like I'm dirty and have to be hidden.

LILY: Wait a second. I didn't put you in the bathroom because I thought you were dirty; I did it to protect you. I tried to tell my father you were there.

BEAR: Oh, please. You know your old man never listens to anything you say even when he shuts up long enough to let you get a word in. If you really wanted to let him know I was there, all you had to do was bring me into the dining room. I promise you he would have noticed me.

LILY: I couldn't do that; he would have hurt you.

BEAR: How can you be so dumb? Your father hurt me? I could have crushed him in a second. You have this habit of forgetting how strong I am because you think it's wrong for anything to be that powerful. It's that good old Catholic upbringing, with all that humility and the meek inheriting the earth stuff. Sure the meek inherit the earth; they get six feet of dirt on top of them, big deal. The strong get the sky. And you know that; you just feel guilty about not wanting to play in the mud like everyone else.

LILY: You know, I don't like you talking about my religion that way.

BEAR: Yeah, I bet you don't. That's why you left me in a bathroom in an all-girls' Catholic school. Adding insult to injury. And you see what happened?

LILY: I was trying to protect you. Someone was after you.

BEAR: Yeah, you know who? You. The part of you that just might be strong enough to get over that "Be humble, don't try to out-glory Jesus" stuff. That's who you tried to protect me from, the part of you that could make me real. Thanks a lot. And look what happened. You lost me. Someone else got your chance at greatness and left you with nothing.

LILY: But I loved you.

BEAR: So what? You kept me chained up, and hidden away from you. You didn't let me do anything or be anything. That kind of love, and five dollars, might buy you a New York subway token these days.

LILY: Are you, and this dream, telling me that it's too late for me to achieve greatness?

BEAR: No, we're telling you that if you don't make some conscious decisions and get a move on it, it will be too late. That's the warning that I mentioned before, about it coming down to either you or me. If you continue to separate yourself from me, you'll lose me completely. Of course, this dream and I are not guaranteeing you greatness, only the possibility of it.

LILY: To unharness you and keep you with me could be very dangerous, especially if I still didn't achieve greatness.

BEAR: Of course it could be dangerous. What made you think it wouldn't be? Everyone else who's achieved greatness, and even many of those who have failed, paid a price in some way. Why should you get a free ride? You're luckier than most just to be having this conversation with me. In the end it doesn't really matter because there will be consequences either way. Now you know everything; the choice is yours.

LILY: One last question. Why are you a bear?

BEAR: Personally, I think it's evidence, solely lacking in other areas of your life, of extraordinarily good taste. I don't know if you remember, but when you were a little kid, you used to make up fantasies and adventures involving your teddy bear and yourself. And you always gave the hero role to the bear. Your parents and the nuns got to you early with that humility garbage, I guess.

LILY: I remember. It sounds like you were there.

BEAR: I've always been there. All these years watching you. It hasn't always been fun. I was hoping you'd discover me on your own, but after almost forty years I began to get worried. I always thought it was a bad sign that you liked seeing me in the zoo, in a cage. I was hoping that you'd be outraged and want to set me free. There are other reasons why I'm a bear, but I'm not going to tell you because that's not the issue and knowing you, you'd make that the issue to avoid dealing with the real one. I'm a bear; and you have choices to make; and now you've been warned. That's it. Goodbye.

LILY: Goodbye. And thank you.

BEAR: You're welcome.

The dreamer was a longtime political activist who had become increasingly involved in real estate and other business investments in the past five years. While still politically involved, she felt her current level of commitment generated only modest achievements; it was not sufficient to accomplish anything truly notable. Political endeavors are among the riskiest, and the dreamer spent a few difficult weeks examining her priorities. Though scared, she was also curious to see what she, and the bear, could do and become. She finally decided to unleash the bear and take her chances. She reduced her business involvements and began focusing her attention on the specific short-term and long-term goals she wanted to accomplish. Her life is not always (or even often) easy, and the financial rewards are substantially less, but she says the exhilaration and peace of mind she gets from knowing she's enacting her highest destiny is priceless. Whenever she gets discouraged she has another conversation with the bear, who affectionately bullies her into continuing.

You can use this exercise on more than one symbol in a dream, and it's highly effective when used in conjunction with other exercises also.

Metaphors

A metaphor is a word, phrase, object, or idea that, in waking life, is consciously chosen to represent another object or idea. It is not meant to be taken literally but rather serves to suggest a similarity between the two. This analogy pinpoints the key characteristics of what is being expressed, and can stir emotions and senses that might not ordinarily be touched, thus evoking the precise affective experience desired. An example is the title of Henry James's "The Beast in the Jungle." The story is not literally about a beast in a jungle, but rather is about the unrecognized, and therefore frightening, aspects of oneself.

As a figure of speech, metaphor resembles a simile. The difference is that a simile uses *like* or *as* so that the comparison is expressed explicitly. For example, "The sky is like a blue carpet" is a simile; "The sky is a blue carpet" is a metaphor. In the latter, the comparison is implied.

Though they lack the literary quality of conscious selection, dreams can be viewed as images and symbols strung together in a series of metaphors that present the unconscious's message in an emotionally impactful way. To understand this message, we have to translate the metaphors.

EXERCISE 4

Translating Metaphors

To facilitate this deciphering process, I've devised the following list of pertinent dream questions. Your answers will give you fundamental information to use as a starting point for the actual translation exercise.

Dream Questions

1. What are the unusual or personally significant images in your dream (e.g., hands made of cloth, your childhood bedside lamp)? What do these mean to you?
2. Who are the other people or dream characters in your dream? Are they strangers or people you know? Do they change identity during the dream?
3. What are the personality traits, actions, or lack of action, of your dream ego (the character in the dream whom you recognize as yourself)?
4. What are the primary emotions in your dream?
5. What are the different points of view in the dream?
6. What are the conflicts and unresolved feelings and situations in the dream?
7. What are the opposites or contrasts in the dream?

8. What is currently happening in your conscious waking life? (This information is especially important; one must understand the context of a dream metaphor in order to appreciate its meaning.)

The final step of the process is actually translating the dream metaphors. This exercise, based on one devised by dream theorist and clinician Montague Ullman, consists of three procedures: breaking down the dream into its individual metaphors, translating each metaphor using the material garnered from answering the dream questions, and putting this information into the context of your present-day life. As with all the exercises, don't try to "force" answers; they will freely tumble out all by themselves if you keep your mind open and nonjudgmental and write spontaneously.

A dreamer decided to translate the metaphors of the following dream:

Lost Baby

I find a baby on the cement floor near a pole in Penn Station. The baby has black hair and looks Asian or Mid-Eastern. I pick it up; it seems to be all right.

I try to notify the proper authorities about the lost baby. It turns into a kitten, and meows and walks down some subway stairs. I walk down the stairs; it's dark and hard to see. I can't see the baby even though I know it's nearby. I don't want it to get lost. A deep, loud, male voice says, "Put that baby back where you found it." "Who are you?" I demand. He says he was sent to tell me this. I say, "Nonsense!" and I pick up the baby.

The dreamer then asked herself the eight dream questions, and got the following information:

Lost Baby (Dream Questions)

1. Images: *Baby*—soft, helpless, dependent, cuddly, needy. *Cement floor*—cold, hard uncomfortable. *Pole*—where I stand when waiting to meet someone. *Penn Station*—where I go to meet my parents. A public place of arrivals and departures, where no one remains very long. *Asian/Middle Eastern*—foreign, exotic, alien, a different culture. *Proper authorities*—law and order, indifferent, tendency to make things worse. *Kitten*—playful, lovable, friendly, inquisitive, needs to be protected. *Subway stairs*—passageway that leads to underground place. *Loud male voice*—intimidating, depersonalized; like voices over public address systems— full of authority and supposedly correct information.
2. Dream Characters: Baby who changes into a kitten; unidentified male voice.
3. Dream ego's personality traits: Protective, gets involved, wants to do the right thing, assertive. Dream ego's actions: I pick up abandoned baby; I try to notify authorities; I walk down subway stairs after the kitten/baby; I stand up to a faceless authority figure; I pick up the baby again and hold it.
4. Primary emotions: *Dream ego*—fear for the safety of something helpless, uncertainty over what to do, defiance toward authority who proposes a bad solution. *Baby*—curiosity. *Male voice*—arrogant authoritativeness, indifference toward baby.

5. Different points of view: *Dream ego*—wanting
to do the right thing. *Baby*—unaware of danger;
helpless. *Male voice*—wanting to be boss, have
orders obeyed.

6. Conflicts/unresolved feelings and situations: Do
I want the responsibility of the baby? What do I
do now with the baby? If the authorities won't
be helpful, who will be?

7. Opposites/contrasts: Helpless baby vs. protective, motherly figure. Helpless baby vs. uncaring male voice. Protecting, motherly figure vs.
uncaring male voice. Taking a protective action
vs. authoritative indifference.

8. Current events in waking life: I have just begun
a new job in a large company. The boss is someone I hardly ever see. I feel a lot of demands are
dumped on me, and then I'm left to fend for
myself. No one seems concerned or helpful.

The dreamer then separated the individual metaphors,
translated them, and placed the information into the context of her waking life, with the following result:

Lost Baby (Translation)

Metaphor: I find a baby on the cement floor
near a pole in Pennsylvania Station.

Translation: I am the baby, helpless and dependent, waiting for someone in a cold, unfriendly place
where people come and go, but don't remain.

Context: I'm working in a big company, where
there are lots of people, each going his or her own
way. No one is particularly friendly. I need help,
and am waiting to connect with someone who will
help me.

Metaphor: The baby has black hair and looks Asian or Middle Eastern.

Translation: I'm foreign, alien, different from other people.

Context: Everyone else in the company seems confident and comfortable; only I feel out of place.

Metaphor: I pick it up; it seems all right.

Translation: I can't see anything wrong with me.

Context: I don't know what it is that makes me feel different from everyone, and I don't know why no one will help me.

Metaphor: I try to notify the proper authorities about the lost baby.

Translation: I try to get outside help for this needy part of me.

Context: I'm nice to the people around me, and do my usual things to try to make friends and get help. So far it hasn't worked.

Metaphor: It turns into a kitten, and meows and walks down some subway stairs.

Translation: This lovable but vulnerable part of myself retreats deep within me.

Context: As I continue to feel ostracized and alone, it gets harder for me to be open and friendly. I don't want to feel my vulnerability.

Metaphor: I walk down the stairs; it's dark and hard to see. I can't see the baby even though I know it's nearby. I don't want it to get lost.

Translation: I am separated from the child in me, and have to go deep inside myself, to where it has retreated, to find it.

Context: Instead of rejecting this vulnerable part of myself, as it seems others have, I have to reach in and get in touch with it.

Metaphor: A deep, loud male voice says, "Put that baby back where you found it."

Translation: The authoritative, emotionally indifferent part of me tells me to ignore the child in me.

Context: Part of me feels that other people must have a good reason for rejecting me, and that I should reject this vulnerable part of me also.

Metaphor: "Who are you?" I demand. He says he was sent to tell me this. I say "Nonsense!" and I pick up the baby.

Translation: I challenge the credibility of this indifferent, rejecting part of myself, and reach out to protect the child in me.

Context: I must not reject or abandon myself even though it seems others are doing that to me. They are not necessarily right in their view of me. I must protect and take care of the vulnerable part of myself.

From doing this exercise, the dreamer saw that she was in danger of taking on the uncaring attitude of the people at work and rejecting her sensitive side. The dream told her that she had to give that frightened aspect of herself the support, assistance, and reassurance it wasn't getting from the outside. The dream not only helped her to accept and feel compassion for the child in her, but also gave her the confidence to feel that she could take care of herself, whether or not she got outside help.

A man received the answer to a difficult personal dilemma from translating the metaphors of this dream:

Pulling the Man through the Sand

I am walking backwards, dragging a heavy, muscular man through the sand. I'm holding him under his arms. He is unconscious. He is much larger than I. I am trying to avoid the large dips in the sand and the violent waves from the ocean. I am not entirely successful; the man, however, is all right.

When I awaken, I realize the burden is too much for me.

The dreamer then answered the questions.

Pulling the Man through the Sand (Dream Questions)

1. Images: *Heavy, muscular man*—a great, monumental person, more like a statue than a human. *Dips of sand*—pitfalls I will stumble into if I don't watch where I am going. *Violent ocean waves*—angry blows.
2. Dream characters: *Man*—unknown, fatherly figure.
3. Dream ego's personality traits: Persevering, caring, doing his best. Dream ego's actions: I'm using all my strength to pull a dead weight. I'm doing everything in my power to protect the unconscious man, but am only partially successful; there are too many outside obstacles that endanger his safety.
4. Primary emotions: *Dream ego*—concern for man's safety, determination to reach a destination, sense of inadequacy because I am too small and weak to protect the man totally. *Man*—unconscious, emotionless.

5. Different points of view: *Dream ego*—I take complete responsibility for his rescue. *Man*—helpless.
6. Conflicts/unresolved feelings: I am not strong enough to do this task right.
7. Opposites/contrasts: My activity vs. the man's passivity. The man's huge, bulky body vs. my much smaller frame. The quiet, unmoving sand vs. the turbulent ocean. The serious mission vs. the vacation-like setting of the beach.
8. Current events in waking life: My wife and I want to get a divorce, but I'm afraid the news will upset my father, who has a heart condition.

The following is his translation of the metaphors:

Pulling the Man through the Sand (Translation)

Metaphor: I am walking backwards, dragging a heavy, muscular man through the sand. I am holding him under his arms.

Translation: I am carrying a great weight and taking total responsibility for it. I am going in the wrong direction.

Context: I am burdened with the knowledge that my wife and I are getting divorced, and I have to decide whether to tell my father.

Metaphor: He is unconscious.

Translation: I am trying to protect a helpless, very ill person who is oblivious to my struggle.

Context: My father is very sick. He doesn't know about my marital problems, and I don't know if he's well enough to take it.

Metaphor: He is much larger than I.

Translation: He is the father, and I am the child.

Context: I still see myself as a child in relationship to my father, and yet am in the position of having to protect him. Because I still see myself as a child with him, I am still seeking his approval and am afraid of disappointing him.

Metaphor: I am trying to avoid the large dips in the sand and the violent waves from the ocean.

Translation: There are many dangers and traps —deep falls and angry blows—around me that I want to avoid.

Context: I am afraid of my father's anger when he finds out that my marriage has failed.

Metaphor: I am not entirely successful; the man, however, is all right.

Translation: At great expense to myself, I manage to bring him to safety. He does not know what I have been through.

Context: The burden of keeping my divorce from my father in order to avoid his anger is too much for me to handle. Protecting myself from his disapproval isn't worth the damage I do to myself in the process.

From doing this exercise, it became clear to the dreamer that he had to tell his father about his impending divorce; keeping it a secret was too self-destructive. He realized that he had deceived himself into believing that his biggest concern was his father's health; rather, it was protecting himself from his father's anger. In trying to please his father and avoid his disapproval, he was holding on to his position of the weak, dependent son.

When working with an individual dream, keep in mind

that the relative importance of dream symbols varies from dream to dream. Some dreams present especially powerful symbols. Other dreams are equally impactful but don't convey their messages through particularly significant images. Your gut instincts are the best judge.

4

Dream Partners and Dream Groups

M*any people find that sharing their*
dreams, either with a partner or in a dream group, adds
new dimensions to their exploration of dream symbolism
and meaning. There are two ways to share dreams:
working with a partner or group on one of your own
dreams, and exploring another person's dream as a way
to gain insights about yourself.

Guidelines

Because they are so personal, dreams should be shared
with certain guidelines in mind. Foremost is understanding (and remembering) that dream sharing is *not* therapy
and should not be treated as such. Dreamwork is a creative activity, however, that in itself provides insights

and directions. Though it's often tempting to interpret other people's dreams and give advice, it's essential to realize that your interpretation will reflect more of your own feelings than the dreamer's. Projecting your own emotions in the process of telling someone else how he or she feels can be confusing, distracting, and potentially harmful to that person. Be aware that any emotions or ideas that come up for you are your own, and respect the dreamer's authority over his or her own dream by focusing your attention on the other person's experience of it, no matter how much it differs from your own. Dreamers must feel free to give full vent to their thoughts and emotions without having to defend or prove them. What a partner or group has to offer dreamers is not answers, but rather a safe, supportive environment within which the dreamers can use the collective imagination present to enhance their experience of their dreams.

When dealing in such vulnerable, personal areas, a commitment of confidentiality is imperative. The sense of trust between dream partners or members of a group ultimately determines the scope and effectiveness of the dreamwork done. While it's important for the partner or group to help the dreamer remain honest and not ignore feelings he or she wants to disown, it's also essential that the dreamer's privacy be respected. Dreamers should feel able to completely express all their feelings without being pressured to reveal or explore an area they are not ready or willing to examine. They must be permitted to terminate a discussion at any point, without having to justify doing so. While maintaining the commitment to honesty, the pervading mood of the partnership or group should be that of gentleness and respect. As dream group members get to know each other better they're able to be more helpful; and the intensity, accuracy, and profundity of their dreamwork increases with time. Members can become so close that they enter into one another's dreams.

Dream partners

Many of you may have informal dream partners without even realizing it; husbands and wives, lovers, close friends, and entire families often regularly share their dreams. How many times have you heard "I had the weirdest dream last night" from those around you? For many people, sharing dreams is something they naturally, automatically do with those close to them. Acknowledging a dream partnership, understanding its dynamics, and maximizing its potential through certain dreamwork techniques can make your dream sharing even more productive and fun.

Many informal (undeclared) dream partners are spouses and lovers. By sharing dreams, you can trace the development of a relationship and spot potential areas of trouble. Spouses and lovers often play major, recurring roles in dreams, and sharing your dream life can enhance your relationship's intimacy. It's important, however, not to judge the dreams of your loved ones or blame them for the ways you might be portrayed; the "you" in their dreams may be a symbol for a part of the dreamer, not you.

A close friend can be the ideal partner; the relationship isn't as sensitive as that between lovers, and your friend will know the context of your life (perhaps better than anyone but you) and thus have the information to

ask the right questions. Once again, remind your friend
to steer clear of the temptation to interpret and give advice.

Though dream sharing is not an institutionalized part
of our culture, many modern parents routinely encourage their children to share their dreams. I know several
families that spend their breakfasts listening to each
other's dreams. Aside from its being fun, one father said
that it helps him keep in touch with his children's emotional development, spot problems or areas of concern,
and enables him really to get to know his children as
separate individuals. Very busy with his career, he finds
that this breakfast ritual helps him maintain a deep connection with his family. When listening to your children's
dreams, it's important not to criticize their dream actions
or thoughts or to try to interpret the dreams; they own
their dreams as much as adults own theirs. Rather, you
should encourage your children to express their feelings
about the dream and discover their own meanings.

Making the time and space to become your child's
"formal" dream partner creates a new, special dimension
to your relationship. You can enhance your children's
creative potential and enjoyment by having them write
stories, draw pictures, make collages, act out (when ap-
propriate) their dreams. You can also help them develop
"dream friends" to assist them in confronting and over-
powering the monsters in their nightmares. Never push
your child to use a particular exercise on a dream. Suggest possibilities, then let the child do whatever feels
right. One of the exercises offered later in this chapter—
experiencing your partner's dream as if it were your
own—can give you insight into what your children are
feeling and how you can best help them. You may not

always be delighted by the way you appear in your children's dreams, but be open to the many possibilities of meaning instead of judging or getting angry. Your children's dreams can be important sources of information about your relationship with them and about important or problematical areas in their lives.

EXERCISE 5
Step Back into Your Dream

In this technique, the dreamer reenters his dream while awake and his partner guides him in further exploration. We don't always understand everything in our initial experience of a dream. By stepping back into it in this way, confusing messages can be clarified, characters and images can be questioned and understood, and positive resolutions can be reached. Some dream theorists object to what they consider to be "tampering with dreams," claiming that the later re-creation isn't a true representation of the dream. However, I feel that the positive resolution of the dream is as intrinsic a creation of the dreamer as the negative, frustrating one. By reaching into their inner resources to devise this alternative outcome, dreamers can discover the hidden solutions to their difficulties.

The dreamer first tells the partner the dream in its entirety and then, in a meditative state, begins retelling it. It's now up to the dream partner to direct the dreamer, asking an occasional pertinent question, such as:

What are you feeling now?

How would you change that aspect of the dream?

What does that image remind you of?

How would you like to deal with that particularly charged or frightening symbol?

The partner can also suggest dream tasks to the dreamer, such as:

Become the other character.

Have a dialogue with the different dream elements.

Amplify the image.

Recreate the ending.

These tasks will be described later in the book.

As you can see, the partner's task requires great sensitivity. Knowing as much as possible about the dreamer and the context of the other's life will enable the partner to guide the dreamer in having the optimal experience of his or her dream. While partners should listen to their own unconscious when working with dreamers, it's essential that they remember that their task is to be involved in the dreamer's experience of the dream and not their own.

A student found this exercise enormously beneficial with the following dream:

Learning to Get What I Want

I am swimming in the water in the Caribbean Islands; the water is warm and beautiful. A sea horse approaches me. It's a beautiful animal, full of joy and wanting to help me. As I stare at it, it suddenly becomes a ferocious monster. I have to get away from it. As I fight off the monster, I make my way toward a sunken ship. Its windows and doors are sealed and there's no way to get in, but I must enter it. I see some scuba divers and yell to them for help. They give me a bomb. I know if I try to use the bomb to get into the sunken ship, it will blow the ship up.

The dreamer told the dream to his partner. The following is a condensed version of his experience of stepping back into the dream, guided by his partner.

Learning to Get What I Want
(Back in the Dream)

DREAMER: I'm swimming in the Caribbean Islands. A sea horse approaches me.

DREAM PARTNER: Talk to the sea horse.

DREAMER: (I): Are you going to change into a monster again?

(SEA HORSE): No. Last time your anger made me become a monster. But now you're speaking to me nicely. If you get on my back, I'll take you to the sunken ship.

DREAMER: I climb on the sea horse's back and he swims toward the ship. Riding him is fun. He drops me off near some scuba divers.

DREAM PARTNER: Before he leaves, ask the sea horse for a gift.

DREAMER: (I): Please give me a gift.

(SEA HORSE): Your gift is this word of advice: Ask the scuba divers how to get into the sunken ship.

DREAMER: I ask the divers how to get into the ship and they give me a password; it sounds like gibberish to me. I say the password and the door to the ship flies open and I can enter.

DREAM PARTNER: How do you feel?

DREAMER: Triumphant and successful. I got what I wanted.

After completing the exercise, the dreamer noted that this experience of the dream differed from his initial one in two major ways. First, instead of arriving at the ship by fighting off a sea monster, he was carried there by the sea horse. Second, the scuba divers, instead of handing him a bomb, gave him a password that provided instant access to the ship. The dreamer saw that he didn't have to be combative or defensive to get what he wanted; on the contrary, he learned that it was more effective to be friendly and express his wish openly. The dreamer had this dream when he (along with several other people) was applying for a choice apartment in the city. From his dream, he saw that his attitude had made the process more contentious than it had to be. "The first time I had the dream," the dreamer reported, "I felt good because I fought the monster instead of being petrified with fear. But now I realize it didn't have to become a monster in the first place." Through stepping back into his dream and reexperiencing it, the dreamer gained an important insight about dealing with other people.

E X E R C I S E   6

Experience Your Partner's Dream as if It Were Your Own

The point of this exercise is to learn something about yourself by working with another person's dream.

The highly subjective insights that can result from working with another person's dream are truly startling.

When you experience another's dream as your own, that person's symbols are transformed into your symbols; it's as if they find the part of your psyche that fits their configuration. This exercise can elicit some of the most revealing and surprising information. Since the dream isn't your own, there is a tendency to approach it with fewer preconceptions. When you begin the exercise having no idea what, if anything, will arise, you can be amazed by the profound, detailed nature of the insights you receive.

But keep in mind that these insights are about you, not your partner. So whenever you feel an uncontrollable urge to tell someone the meaning of his or her dream, beware of projecting your own personality onto that other person. Remember that the purpose of this exercise is to learn something about *yourself*.

The most effective way to swap dreams with a partner is for both to work on the same dream so that you can compare experiences afterward. Write out your partner's dream in the first person, as you would with one of your own, then jointly select an exercise or combination of exercises to do. Let your instinct and experience guide you in your choice.

A husband and wife who wanted to strengthen their relationship worked on the following dream of the husband:

Exercising Woman

I'm standing at the bottom of a hill, looking up at the lone, isolated house at the top. There are no entrances into the house. I have X-ray vision and can see into the house. On the top floor, in the bedroom, a woman is exercising. She knows I'm watching her and is annoyed, but continues doing her exercises anyway.

Both the dreamer and his wife wrote out the dream in the first person, then they decided to use the technique of writing the dream from the other character's point of view;[1] in this case, from the exercising woman's perspective. The following is the dreamer's experience:

Exercising Woman's Point of View (Dreamer)

I'm in the top-floor bedroom of my secluded house. I worked very hard to get this place. I specifically designed my home for privacy and protection; only I can get in. I feel safe and secure in my fortress. I enjoy exercising, feeling my muscles stretch and watching my strength and endurance grow. It makes me feel powerful.

Then I feel someone looking at me. I see a man at the bottom of the hill looking up at me; somehow he's able to see through the house. He watches me exercise, and I get mad. The nerve of him! How rude! Some people's manners . . . I'm contemptuous of him but I won't let him affect what I'm doing; that little mosquito at the bottom of the hill can't touch my life. I continue to exercise, but I glower at him so that he knows that I know he's watching me. I assert my power; I show him I can outlast him and not alter my life. I will continue to ignore him and focus my life on myself.

The dreamer's wife wrote the following version of his dream:

Exercising Woman's Point of View (Dream Partner)

I'm imprisoned alone, condemned to repeat a task for eternity unless someone frees me. But no one can see me in this house.

Suddenly, after centuries, I sense a presence. A man, at the bottom of the hill, can miraculously see through the house. He can see me! He must come up here and free me; this is my one chance. I wait for him to come up the hill to the house but he doesn't move, he just stands and stares. I wish I could wave to him or smile, anything to get him to come up and rescue me. But my body only moves in this one prescribed way, and the years of torment have frozen my face into a grimace. I'm terrified he'll leave, thinking that I don't want him to come up here. I wish he'd make some sign to me, but he just stares.

The dreamer and his partner each received individually tailored messages from the same dream. The dreamer realized that he was concerned that his way of expressing interest in a woman could be viewed as intrusive and result in him being rejected. His wife saw that she wanted to be rescued from the barriers she put up that inhibited her from getting close to people. Two entirely different, highly introspective experiences resulted from one person's dream. By sharing their experiences, the husband and wife were able to reach a better understanding of one another.

E X E R C I S E   7
Draw a Dream and Tell the Story

Another way to work with a dream partner is for one person to draw a key scene or image from his or her dream and let the other tell the story of the dream by looking at the picture. Dreams are primarily pictures, and visual expressions of them tend to elicit sudden insights and expose new facets of the dreamer. Two people's perceptions of the same picture can be as individually revealing as their interpretations of the same dream, and the results can be enlightening to both the dreamer and the partner. It's best if the dreamer says very little about the dream until after the partner shares the experience.

Two women, an artist, and a writer, frequently practice this exercise; they find that it enhances their work as well as sparking personal discoveries. The following is an example of how they've used the exercise. The artist had this dream:

Resurrection

I'm being chased by a monster through a field. Ahead of me, I see a lake. Somehow, I know the monster can't swim. I run toward the lake; the monster is on my heels because it knows it has to get me before I reach the lake. I feel that it's scared of what will happen if it doesn't catch me, as if it will be punished in some way. I dive into the lake right before the monster grabs my shoulder. It cries as it watches me swim away. I feel kind of sorry for it.

As I swim, I meet up with an old man. I know he's my father, even though my father died at age thirty, when I was very young. I get scared; I wonder if this means I've died. Maybe the monster had been trying to rescue me, and that's why it cried. I cry as I ask my father if I'm dead. He reassures me and says no, that I'm not dead, because I'm not me any longer. I'm him as a young man, being given a second chance for life. I look down at my body and see that I am now a man. I stretch out my arms and slowly rise out of the water.

The dreamer drew this picture of her dream (Figure 1) and showed it to her dream partner, who wrote the following "dream."

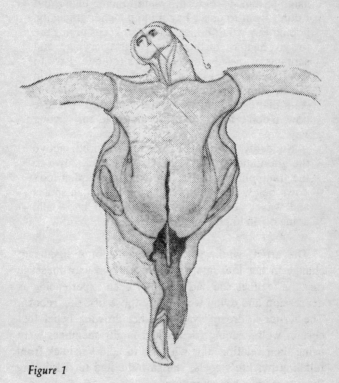

Figure 1

Life on a Trampoline

I'm at my parent's house with my childhood best friend, Fay. We are adults, but we are dressed up as children. We go into the backyard to play, and discover a trampoline. I start jumping on it, bouncing up and down in different positions, clowning around to make Fay laugh.

A man appears, and talks to me in soft, gentle tones. He encourages me to jump higher and higher. Fay doesn't trust him, and warns me not to listen to him. I feel torn; I want to jump higher but I don't want to upset Fay. I jump higher gradually, hoping Fay won't notice. The man keeps urging me to go higher, further. Fay starts crying, and screams at me to stop before it's too late. I try to stop but I can't; I'm out of control, hurtling up in the air with incredible velocity. I'm not frightened. As a matter of fact, I'm secretly pleased, because now I don't have to feel responsible for hurting Fay.

Suddenly, I fly out of the earth's orbit, above the gravitational field. I don't come back down to the trampoline but just keep going upward. I look down below me. Fay is crying, but the man smiles and waves. I'm elated but nervous; I know I'm going on an important journey.

The artist, who was in the middle of a significant change in her life, interpreted her dream as a message that the feelings she had currently been experiencing as depression and dying were really those of being reborn. The writer's "dream" validated her growing belief that certain well-meaning friends and family members were using their relationships with her to hold her back from fulfilling her life's goals; she saw she had to risk losing them to pursue her aspirations.

Though their dreams were quite different, the dream partners were struck by the fact that they both received major insights regarding their present waking lives through merely drawing and creating a dream.

Dream groups

*As previously mentioned, dream sharing has been an in-*tegral part of certain primitive and ancient cultures. The benefits and pleasures of sharing dreams are evidenced today by the many private dream groups that have been formed in the United States. Cutting across all cultural lines and distinctions, these groups have ranged from housewives to improvisational acting classes to schizophrenic adolescents. Dreamworker Jeremy Taylor started a prison dream group at San Quentin several years ago; even though they were disobeying the rules, the armed guards that accompanied him couldn't resist getting involved in the group and contributing their own dreams. (The desire to talk with others about our dreams is a basic human drive.) Taylor discovered that many of the guards had suffered the classic children's nightmare about being devoured by demonic giants. He eventually learned that many of the guards, as well as the convicts, had had abused childhoods.[2]

If you want to join an established dream group, try contacting a church, library, or school, or answering a magazine or newspaper advertisement. One consideration is whether you want to become part of a group led by an expert or a group that is leaderless. A good leader, with professional training, can be an invaluable catalyst and guide, able to pinpoint vital areas of concern and keep the group focused, constructive, and working smoothly. An inexperienced leader, however, may push dreamers into accepting his or her interpretations of their dreams instead of helping them discover their own; this leader uses his knowledge to intimidate or manipulate, and generally upsets what should be an atmosphere of equality and mutual respect. Although a leaderless group can create a suitable atmosphere and devise a structure specifically designed for its members, it can also lose its focus, become a battleground for opposing wills, and get stuck when confused.

You can also start your own dream group. Word of mouth is usually sufficient to get together a group, but you can also post notices at your church, library, YMCA, or similar public building. Ideally, dream groups should be composed of four to six members and meet in regular two-hour sessions. At your first meeting you should decide how often the group will meet. A serious commitment to regular attendance is important; a group that meets twice a month with all its members present is far more effective than one that meets weekly with only sporadic attendance. It's a good idea for each member to share what he or she hopes to get from the group, and the first meeting is the time to handle potentially divisive topics like refreshments, smoking, and meeting places. Though it's important for the group to remain flexible, plan on working with only one or two dreams per session to ensure that each dream is given all the time it needs. It's best to work with short, recent dreams, and members will find it useful to take notes during the exercises.

All the guidelines for dream partners are applicable to dream groups as well. Confidentiality is of utmost importance. Inviting visitors to meetings is not recommended, and it must be clear that whatever is discussed in the group is not to be mentioned elsewhere. And there should be no doubt in anyone's mind that dream groups are *not* group therapy.

There are many ways for a dream group to work with dreams, from acting them out like plays to letting each person select a dream conflict or problematical situation, resolve it through one of the exercises outlined in this book, and share the experience with the other group members. Each member can choose a specific action to carry out during the week, based upon the new awareness gained from the dream, and report the results of this action when the group meets again. Actualization, after all, is the key to change.

Montague Ullman, a leading dream therapist and clinician, has developed an exercise that is enormously useful in eliciting the maximum benefits from the group's collective imagination.

E X E R C I S E   8

Montague Ullman's Dream Group Exercise

This technique, which entails each group member's experiencing the selected dream as if it were his or her own, can be broken down into these six steps:[3]

1. The dreamer tells the dream in its entirety without giving any interpretations. It's helpful if the dreamer has previously written down the dream and then reads it aloud to the group so that there's no question or argument over its content. The dreamer recites the dream without interruption from the group, being aware of all the feelings that arise as it is told. The narrator needs to pay special attention to the feelings or parts of the dream that he or she is tempted to disown or gloss over.
2. When the dreamer finishes, the group then asks ques-

tions about any of the dream's contents that are un-
clear. These should not be interpretive questions but
rather those regarding the details of the dream itself.

3. After all the questions are answered, each member of
the group discusses the dream as if it were that
member's own, sharing all the emotions and associations that came up for him or her. In this way, all
group members gain the benefit of doing their own
dreamwork as well as helping the chosen dreamer
reach a deeper self-understanding. It must be abso-
lutely clear, however, that each person is sharing a
personal experience of the dream, and not the
dreamer's experience. It's useful to begin each recita-
tion of the dream with: "When I had this dream, I
felt..." The dreamer listens silently, understanding
that the recited dream reflects the point of view of the
speaker; the value of listening to other peoples'
dreams lies in the associations that may be triggered
in the dreamer's awareness. The dreamer can make
notes of comments to which he or she particularly
reacts, but now is not the time to respond to them.

4. After everyone has given a rendition of the dream, the
dreamer then reacts to what he or she has heard.
Some of the associations will be right on target and
others will be off, but even those that don't corre-
spond to the dreamer's can trigger other ideas. The
group members shouldn't try to justify or defend their
experiences; their goal is not to second-guess the
dreamer but rather to share their own feelings.

5. The group then asks the dreamer for any specific life
circumstances that may relate to the dream, and
about any imagery or interpretations that come to the
dreamer's mind. The group avoids pressure tactics
that will get the dreamer to reveal more than is comfortable.

6. The dreamer concludes the exercise by telling the
group what he or she has learned from this experience.

This technique opens the way for many different associations, interpretations, and ideas. The group must not

try to force the dreamer into having some kind of a breakthrough or insist on details that the dreamer wants to keep private. The real insights may come days or weeks later. The dream group's task is to enable the dreamer to experience the dream fully, and let the dreamer decide where to go from there.

The following illustrates how a group utilized this technique. The example is greatly condensed—the actual procedure took close to an hour—but it demonstrates the way the process works. The dreamer is A, and the other members of the group are B, C, D, and E. The dreamer started by reading her dream from her dream journal.

Dream within a Dream

I am in my apartment, talking on the phone to a friend, when my other phone rings. I answer it, and am unnerved to hear my old boyfriend Paul's voice. He greets me in his typically upbeat, slick way, asking me how I am. For some reason, I tell him that I dreamed about him the night before. That's not true; he wasn't in my dream, but I say that anyway. He asks me what the dream was about, and I tell him that I dreamed I was standing in the middle of a baseball diamond in the center of town, and he was with me. He asks me what I think the dream means, and I tell him that I think it means that I have my life centered and together even though I still miss him.

Group members then asked some clarifying questions regarding the dream's content.

B: Did you make up the whole baseball diamond dream or just the part about him being in the dream?

A: The baseball diamond dream was real, but he wasn't in it.

C: What was his response to being in your dream?

A: He was pleased, and consequently very interested in the dream.

D: What were your thoughts as you told him the dream?

A: I was surprised that I was going through the effort of making up this lie, nervous that he might somehow discover he wasn't really in my dream, and aware that I was giving him important information regarding my feelings for him.

E: How did you *really* feel about your baseball diamond dream?

A: I felt important and exhilarated, but I didn't want him to know that.

Then each member of the group talked about the dream as if it were his or her own.

B: When I had this dream, I felt torn between liking Paul and knowing he was no longer part of my life.

C: When I had this dream, I felt I wanted to be the center of attention but had to disguise that desire by pretending someone else was in the dream because I didn't deserve to be the center of attention.

D: When I had this dream, I felt pressured to boost Paul's ego by making him feel important even though he had hurt me and made me feel unimportant.

E: When I had this dream, I felt I was faking intimacy. I felt I was really severing our connection even though it appeared that I was trying to establish one.

The dreamer then responded to the group's experiences.

A: I was aware that even though I liked him, he wasn't really in my life. And it bothered me, because the child in me has a hard time accepting that I can't always get what I want. With Paul it was especially hard because I knew he liked me too, but it wasn't enough to enable him to be a real part of my life. And as much as I intellectually understood all the reasons for this, on a gut level I couldn't understand it and so I couldn't let go. And I did feel pressured to make him feel important, as if that would make him feel more secure and less afraid of getting involved. But as I did that—lied to make him feel important—I realized that I was faking a connection with him, and it did make me feel cut off from him. Toward the end of the dream I started wondering why, if he was so important, he wasn't really in my dream.

The group then questioned A about the circumstances surrounding the dream and her interpretation of the key images.

B: What's the history of your relationship with Paul?
A: Two years ago, I dated him for six months. I liked him a lot, but broke up with him because he couldn't commit to a relationship, not just with me but with anyone. Three months ago, I ran into him

at the wedding of two mutual friends. We had a good time together at the wedding, and we started seeing each other again, about once every two weeks, as friends. After a couple of dates we started sleeping together, but on a very casual basis. Even though I've implicitly agreed to the casual nature of our relationship, I now find myself wanting more from him. It's very frustrating because I haven't met anyone I've liked half as much in years.

C: How did you feel when you awoke from the dream?

A: I really missed him a lot.

D: What happened that day that might have contributed to the dream?

A: I saw Paul for lunch, and we shared a pizza. I told him that it was fine to order it with mushrooms and anchovies, the way he wanted it, even though I only like pizza plain and anchovies make me gag.

E: What does a baseball diamond mean to you?

A: It's an enclosed, protected area.

A then talked about what she learned from this exercise.

A: I feel that much of my relationship with Paul is based on the false pretense that I feel OK about seeing him in such an uncommitted way. I see that doing this establishes a superficial connection with him, but in reality it cuts me off from him even further because it's a lie. In a sense, I'm a lie when I'm with him. I think I awoke feeling sad because I realized that our relationship was over, whether or not I continued to see him.

Not only did the dreamer find this exercise enormously useful in clarifying a confusing relationship, but several members of the group said that their experiences of the dream gave them insights into their feelings about their own love relationships.

Dreams are unique gifts; through sharing them, we offer and receive new opportunities for self-knowledge.

PART TWO

Dream Theories

The Legacy of Freud

In the beginning . . .

*T*he theories of Sigmund Freud have become so ingrained, albeit not always accepted, in our popular culture that it's easy to forget how truly revolutionary they were at the time when they were introduced. At the beginning of the twentieth century, the medical establishment regarded dreams as meaningless hallucinations. It was against this background that Freud, a neuropathologist scorned by the medical establishment for his views on infantile sexuality, wrote and published the innovative *The Interpretation of Dreams*. Much of his dream theory was based on a comprehensive study of his own dreams in the late 1890s. Radically disagreeing with prevailing medical opinions on dreams, he considered them extremely important; dreams, he claimed, were the "royal road to the unconscious." It would be a major understatement to say the medical world didn't jump on his bandwagon, and he has remained a controversial figure ever since, both exalted and repudiated.

It has been fashionable among many to deride Freud and dismiss his views out of hand. Certainly some of his theories have been discarded or diminished in importance; however, many of his concepts do remain the foundation of modern psychological thought. As a colleague of mine commented, "I agree with Freud on almost nothing, but I know I wouldn't be here if it weren't for him." Freud gave us a remarkable gift: access to the unconscious, with dreams as the chief source of insight and information. And despite the questionable validity of *some* of his ideas, it's acknowledged that certain Freud techniques, such as the free association method for working with dreams, are enormously useful. When assessing Freud and his theoretical contributions, it is important to keep two things in mind. One, because he was the first Western scientist to approach the study of human behavior from this perspective, it was inevitable that he would oversimplify or err in some areas; even today there is no one universally agreed-upon school of psychological theory. And two, he and his patients were all products of the severely sexually repressed Victorian society; thus his theories may have been more accurate in that historical and cultural framework. No matter how you feel about Freud and his ideas, it's fascinating and worthwhile to understand the origins of Western dream theory.

Dream = repressed sexual desire

*A dream, Freud asserted, was the fulfillment of a re-*pressed infantile wish. For the most part, these biological and instinctual wishes (stemming from ages one to three) were sexual. Unacceptable to the conscious mind and therefore repressed, these desires lay dormant in the unconscious until a dream expressed them in a symbolic form. Thus the dream both discharged the dreamer's unconscious excitation and yet still protected his sleep by disguising the wish so that he wouldn't awaken in shame or alarm.

Modern research has disproved Freud's belief in dreams as guardians of sleep, demonstrating that they are physiological processes. However, this error in no way invalidates his work in interpreting the content of dreams.

In analyzing dreams, Freud made a distinction between the manifest dream and the latent dream. The manifest dream was the actual dream itself; it served to disguise the message of the latent dream, which was the repressed wish from the unconscious. Freud discovered that a patient could eventually expose and understand his latent dream by free-associating to various elements of the manifest dream. Freud formulated his interpretation of the dream from the sum total of these free associations, using a complex variety of procedures to decode the dream's message. Later in this chapter, I will demonstrate an exercise, based on free association, that can enable you to understand a seemingly incomprehensible dream.

Sexual symbolism

Freud's first step in examining a dream was to look for
the sexual significance in the dream's symbolism. Whatever was in the form of a receptacle—such as boxes,
bowls, and houses—or was enclosing—such as rooms
and tunnels—represented the vagina, as did mouths,
ears, and eyes. That which was oblong or suggested pen-
etration—sticks, knives, umbrellas, pencils, nail files
(which suggested rubbing up and down), along with
hands, feet, and the number three—represented the
penis. Animals such as fish, snails, cats, mice, and
snakes, as well as complicated machinery and landscapes, were also symbols for the genitals. Even children in a dream meant genitals; Freud explained that the
people of his era often modestly referred to their sexual
organs as their "little ones," and, of course, little ones
are also children.

The sex act, as well as the organs, was also well represented in dreams. People who dreamed of walking up
and down steps, stairs, and ladders were really dreaming
of having sex. Playing with a child was not the innocent
act it appeared, but rather was masturbation. Hair cutting, teeth falling out, and baldness all meant castration.

Freud, borrowing this example from Wilhelm Stekel,
discerned moral messages in dreams based on whether
the individual dreamed of going to the right or to the left.
If a person dreamed he was going right, it meant he was
following the path of righteousness, marriage, or inter-
course with a prostitute (which in Freud's time was considered honorable behavior for a gentleman). If he
dreamed of going to the left, it signified he unconsciously

could be headed toward crime, homosexuality, incest, or perversion.

In his earliest years, Freud believed an analyst could, to some extent, analyze a dream without knowing the patient's associations. Later he revised his opinion, conceding that a particular symbol could, and often did, have more than one meaning; indeed, it could have several meanings. He then declared that the correct interpretation of the symbol came from its context. Thus, despite his obsession with sexuality, he still insisted that the patient's associations were important in the translation of the symbol. And it was the obligation of the analyst to adopt a combined technique based on both the dreamer's associations and on the interpreter's knowledge of symbols.

Censorship in dreams

Symbolism was only one of the censorship processes, which Freud labeled "dream-work," that transformed and disguised the unacceptable sexual desires of the latent dream into the tolerable content of the manifest dream. The other means of dream censorship were *condensation, displacement,* and *secondary revision.*

According to Freud, *condensation* was the compression of the true dream into a brief, laconic form. Thus a number of different people in the dreamer's life would be represented by a single dream character, several life situations would be compressed into one situation, and a variety of wishes from different periods of the dreamer's life would be expressed by a single wish. However, there was a common trait in the different people, a common situation in all the situations, and a common wish in all the wishes; these, he believed, were revealed through free association. The deepest wish behind all the others is the infantile wish, and it is responsible for the formation of the dream. Other aspects of the condensation process are the reversal of an emotion into its opposite and multiple determination, which is the repetition of dream elements.

Displacement serves to mask the dream's true intent by attaching the strong emotional response to dream content of minor significance while the important content, to which it truly belongs, is virtually ignored. Freud gives the example of an elderly man who was laughing so hard in his sleep that his wife woke him up in alarm. The elderly man had dreamed that he was lying in bed when a gentleman whom he knew appeared in the room. The dreamer made many attempts to turn on the light but failed each time. Then his wife tried, but, feeling self-conscious in her negligee, she gave up and returned to bed. This struck the old man so funny that he laughed until he woke up. However, the next day he complained of depression and a headache. The depression and headache became understood when the true meaning of the dream became clear. In the dream, the gentleman represented death; the dreamer's unrestrained laughter replaced the sobbing and weeping that he actually might have expressed at the idea of his own impending death.[1] Therefore, in this dream, the dream's disguise was achieved by reversing the emotion into its opposite and attaching it to the wife's embarrassing dilemma rather than to its true cause.

It's human nature to want to put an experience into intelligible order. *Secondary revision* is our attempt to do that with our dreams; an example is filling in gaps in the dream so that it no longer seems absurd and disconnected. In doing this, though, we destroy the dream's true meaning and significance. The distortion of secondary revision can occur just in the recalling and retelling of a dream, unless the dream is written down immediately. That's why it's so important to keep a pen and pad by your bed.

In regarding dreams in the Freudian context of expressions of repressed desires, it's impossible not to wonder how nightmares and bad dreams fit into the paradigm. After all, what wish is being fulfilled in a dream, let's say, of someone we desire rejecting us, or of being publicly humiliated or attacked? Freud perceived these dreams as punishment dreams; we feel guilty for our wishes and so punish ourselves with failure and danger. He explained dreams in which a beloved person dies as evidencing unconscious hostile feelings or an unconscious desire to be rid of the person.

E X E R C I S E 9

Free Association

Although some of his theories have been subsequently altered or discarded, there's little debate over the effectiveness of free association, the technique Freud developed to get to the true wish behind the disguise. The following exercise is based on the principles of free association and can enable you to uncover an elusive dream's meaning.

After writing out the entire dream, select the pithiest paragraph. List every word of it on the left side of the page and write your associations to it—whatever pops into your mind—opposite it, on the right side of the page. Your associations can be words or phrases. Don't force ideas; if an association to a word doesn't come, skip it and go on and then return to it later. When you've finished listing the associations, rewrite the dream segment using only the associations.

A patient used this technique on a recurring dream she'd had since childhood and uncovered a long-repressed feeling.

The German Shepherd

I am on a stairway. A German shepherd is coming up the stairs toward my cat. I go charging down the stairs, screaming at the dog to chase it away. I succeed.

She then listed the key words and her associations to them.

Key Words	Associations
I	me, eye
am	exist, live
on	where
stairway	up and down, wood banister
German	rough, tough, mean, tyrannical, hard, killer
German shepherd	dog, watch out, be careful, bite
shepherd	peaceful, overseer, watch over
coming	emerging, burst, sperm
up	inside

stairs	leading to
toward	watch out, careful, thrust
my	mine, belonging to, oh my my
cat	furry, raw meat
I	eye, aye aye
go	get out
charging	penis, army, father's fist
down	soft, abyss, falling, dark, hole
stairs	falling, getting hurt
screaming	help, screech, frightening
at	where
dog	bark, dirty, don't touch, wet
to	leading, taking
chase	something being attacked, tracked down, fearful
it	nothing, neuter
away	gone, into distance, sad, alone
I	aye aye, sir
succeed	fail, win, accomplish

She then rewrote the dream, using only her associations:

The German Shepherd (Associations)

Eye exist where up and down. A rough, tough, mean, tyrannical, killer, be careful, an overseer who watches over and is peaceful, bursts inside, leading to thrusting oh my my furry raw meat. Aye aye, get out penis, army, father's fist, soft abyss, falling, dark hole getting hurt, help where dirty, don't touch, wet, taking, something being attacked, nothing neuter into distance, sad, alone. And aye aye sir, fail.

After doing this exercise, the dreamer was flooded with the memories of her father's explicit sexual desire for her when she was a small child. It had been so traumatic that she had completely blocked this awareness for forty years, and it only surfaced in this camouflaged dream. One major reason this patient entered therapy was to deal with her inability to sustain any kind of intimate relationship with a man. Recalling these memories was extremely painful, but the revelation also offered a sense of relief. All the psychic energy used to bury this knowledge was now released, and her therapy could now help her make peace with her past and go forward.

This exercise is especially useful with dreams that seem nonsensical, or "meaningless." A woman considered the following dream absurd and meaningless until she rewrote it from her free associations.

Rescued in the Snowstorm

The moon falls out of the sky. There is an enormous snowstorm. My mother picks me up and carries me through a path that is being formed in the snow, which is four feet high. She is rescuing both herself and me. I think I am made of cloth. I have six eyes in my forehead.

She then listed her associations to it.

Rescued in the Snowstorm (Associations)

Key Words	Associations
moon	shadow, mystery
falls	bruises, defeats, fails
out	unloved, ostracized

out of	was born to, comes from
sky	unattainable, everything, all desire
enormous	overwhelming, huge monster, destruction
snow	cold, pretty but mean, hypocritical, dangerous, not to be trusted
storm	power, beyond good and evil
my	all I own is myself, my mind
mother	want more, never enough love
picks	not chosen, rejected
me	surface with nothing inside, alone, everything and nothing
up	success, away from danger
carries	burdened with
carries me	out of control, dumped at any time
through	danger on either side
path	rocky road
being	is, alive, lucky
formed	birth, limits, loss of endless possibility
in	deep, sex, intimate
snow	barrier
is	undeniable
four	one left out
feet	ugly
high	attainment, success
she	softness, love, cocoon
is rescuing	erasing barriers, not safe
both	everything, abundance, no need for choice
herself	not mine
me	alone, no boundaries, either impotent or omnipotent
I	sight, brain, perception

think	all-important, best, limitless
I am	notice me, not invisible
made	outer material, separate from inside
of	belonging to, not isolated
cloth	loose threads, pliable, can twist, strong in one way but weak in another, can be ripped but not pulled
I have	certainty, security
six	a crowd, too many to be alone with
eyes	intensity, perception, control
forehead	center of operations, power

This was the rewritten dream:

Rescued in a Snowstorm (Rewritten)

The shadow mystery bruises unloved come from all unattainable desire. There is overwhelming destructive, pretty but mean, hypocritical power, beyond good and evil. My mind wants more, not enough love, rejects alone surface with nothing inside success, and burdened with, can be dumped at any time danger on either side a rocky road that is limits, loss of endless possibility, deep, intimate the barrier which is one left out, ugly, attainment. Love, cocoon is erasing barriers, no need for choice, abundance not mine and alone, no boundaries, either impotent or omnipotent. Brain perception best limitless notice me outer material separate from inside belonging to loose threads, pliable, strong in one way and weak in another, can be ripped but not pulled. Certainty, too many to be alone with intensity, perception, control in my center of operations, power.

The dreamer, an ambitious middle-aged lawyer, had this dream at a time when her career was thriving, but at the expense of her marriage. Her rewritten dream instantly struck her as a cry from her emotions for attention and a timely warning from her unconscious that, no matter what her fears about love and intimacy, she would never feel satisfied with just career success; she needed love also. This insight gave her a new appreciation of the value and importance of her marriage that led to a new commitment to give it the attention and care that it deserved. The dreamer remarked that after this dream experience she never considered a dream "meaningless" again.

As you can see, this technique presents its messages in a barrage of hard-hitting ideas and images. Both dreamers reported that their rewritten dreams evoked powerful feelings in them; one described it as "feeling, experiencing, the dream's message as well as understanding it." It is precisely this, feeling our unconscious's truths, that opens the way for emotional growth.

6

Jung's Blueprint for Personal Growth

Freud and Jung: a parting of the ways

*A*fter Freud, the next man to have a monumental impact on psychological theory and therapeutic treatment in the Western world was C. G. Jung. The great Swiss psychologist believed the individual could become whole only through understanding and accepting his or her unconscious. Dreams and dream symbols were the keys to this knowledge, and Jung's therapy was largely based on the analysis of dreams.

Jung was initially a disciple of Freud. He first read Freud's *The Interpretation of Dreams* as a very young man. Later he realized that his ideas were closely linked to Freud's; he was particularly impressed by Freud's theory of repression. Even after he parted from Freud, Jung believed that Freud's greatest contribution to civilization was his discovery of the way to the unconscious, with dreams being the major source of information regarding its contents. When they met in 1907, Jung was thirty-two and Freud, fifty-one. Partly due to the age difference and Jung's idolization of him, Freud couldn't resist considering Jung as his son. But, as often happens between fathers and sons, the son eventually broke away from the father's domination. After five years, Jung parted from Freud and the psychoanalytic movement; Freud was deeply embittered.

Where did their relationship go wrong? First, although Jung agreed with Freud's theory of repression, he couldn't accept the idea that sexual trauma was at the root of every repression. According to Jung, Freud denied anything that was spiritual, and suspected every spiritual expression to be repressed sexuality. When Freud implored Jung to carry forth his ideas about sexuality as dogma, Jung backed off. He felt Freud had no objectivity when it came to this issue.

To Jung, libido was psychic energy, not merely sexuality, as Freud believed. Sexuality, he felt, was a fundamental expression of psychic wholeness but by no means the sole one. Rather than accepting Freud's theory that sexual desire emanated from incestuous feelings, he maintained that people essentially longed for the security, protection, and mutual love and trust ideally expressed in the parental relationship.

The collective unconscious

Jung's theory of the collective unconscious, like many of his other ideas, was contained in a dream.

Jung dreamed he was in an unfamiliar house, but knew it was his own house. The house had two stories; Jung was on the upper floor, a salon with rococo furni-

ture and valuable old paintings on the walls. Wondering
what was on the floor below, Jung walked downstairs to
a fifteenth- or sixteenth-century setting. The rooms were
dark, and the furnishings medieval. He noticed a heavy
door, opened it, and descended a stone stairway to the
cellar. The cellar had a beautifully vaulted room from the
Roman period. The floor was made up of stone slabs and
in one of these slabs was a ring. Jung pulled the ring and
lifted the slab, exposing another stairway. He walked
down the narrow stone steps to a low cave cut into the
rock. The floor was covered with dust, scattered bones,
and broken pottery; it looked like the remnants of a
primitive civilization. There, Jung found two partially
disintegrated human skulls.[1]

Freud attempted to analyze this dream, asking Jung
whom the skulls represented, and toward whom Jung
had death wishes. Jung could not accept this line of interpretation, but kept his thoughts secret at that time. He
rejected Freud's postulation that the dream was a disguise of the unconscious's true meaning; he believed
dreams didn't disguise but rather expressed the unconscious directly. According to Jung, the tricks of the conscious mind couldn't intervene in the natural processes
of the unconscious.

Jung subsequently made his own interpretation of this
dream. To him, it represented the successive layers of
consciousness. And while agreeing with Freud on the
existence of a personal unconscious, Jung went further
and discovered the deepest level of the mind: the collective unconscious. He determined that each of us has
within us the entire history of the race. This collective
unconscious contains all human experience since the beginning of mankind. These fundamental experiences and
beliefs have been expressed in myths, legends, fairy

tales, and religions throughout history.

Jung transcended Freud's purpose of curing neuroses. A dream, he believed, could reveal the roots of a neurosis and also show the prognosis and course of treatment. In addition, a dream could denote not only wish fulfillment but also hunger, anxiety, transcendental truths, philosophy, advice, memories, fantasies, precognitions, telepathic visions, and more. According to Jung, dreams contained the blueprint for personal growth and thus were essential in the quest for self-knowledge.

Compensation

A major principle of Jung's dream theory is compensation, the belief that dreams present thoughts and emotions that have been overlooked and that may, in fact, be the opposite of what the dreamer is consciously feeling. Compensation occurs when a person goes too far in one direction; the dream serves to remind the person that something is being ignored and that the dreamer needs to create more of a balance in his or her feelings or life.

Jung thought the major fallacy in the commonly held conception of the unconscious was that its contents, whether positive or negative, were permanent and unalterable. Instead, he viewed the psyche as a neutral, fluid, self-regulating system, predisposed to maintaining its sense of balance like the body itself. Thus every process that goes too far inevitably evokes an opposite, compensatory process. Jung classified people according to two sets of paired functions: intellect-emotion and sensation-intuition. In every person, one characteristic of each set is predominant or conscious, and the other is unconscious. Thus someone is either primarily intellectual or emotional, a sensation type or intuitive. In addition, there is the polarity of introversion and extroversion, concepts that were coined by Jung. Dreams create a balance of personality by bringing to the foreground the unconscious functions. For example, a person who is an extroverted intellectual may find that his dreams reveal his introverted, emotional side. Jung was convinced that this compensatory relationship between the conscious and the unconscious was "one of the best-proven rules of dream interpretation."[2]

Jung illustrates his concept by reporting a compensation dream that chided him for being too critical of someone. He dreamed he saw a castle on a hill. The castle had a high tower with a balustrade, and an elegant woman sat upon the balustrade. Looking up so high caused Jung to develop a pain in his neck. He saw that the woman was one of his patients. When Jung awoke, he realized that he put this patient so high up in his dreams because he consciously looked down on her; she was nicknamed "the great whore of Babylon." The dream made Jung aware that the patient was not a bad woman, but that he had been a bad doctor.[3]

Compensation dreams can be puzzling until we understand their message. A patient was enraged that his girlfriend had flirted with another man. For two weeks he had recurring dreams about apologizing to his girlfriend for his jealousy and accepting her apologies. He'd wake up after every dream, livid with himself for apologizing to her. It infuriated him that he kept having these dreams. He finally realized that his anger was way out of proportion to the situation, and that his psyche was reestablishing a balance by having these dreams. When he talked with his girlfriend and resolved the situation, the dreams went away.

Compensation dreams can also provide pleasures that are consciously lacking. One dreamer who experienced this was a patient who said that for a long time she'd been feeling that she would never meet anyone she would really love. After months of loneliness and disappointment, she reported a dream in which she met a wonderful man and felt all the joy and pleasure that comes from an intimate, loving relationship. She awoke from the dream feeling energized and optimistic. Her despair and hopelessness had thrown her off balance, and her unconscious helped her regain her emotional equilibrium by providing her with some of the feelings she needed to experience.

As you can see, familiarity with the dreamer's waking thoughts is essential in dream interpretation. You can't know what the unconscious is responding to or compensating for if you don't know what the dreamer is consciously experiencing. When you're working with a dream, be aware of how it might reflect your conscious situation, and note if it's pointing out an imbalance. Jung always found it helpful to ask "What conscious attitude does this compensate?" when about to interpret a dream.[4]

E X E R C I S E   1 0

Amplification

Like Freud, Jung believed the key to self-awareness and growth lay in making the unconscious conscious. Jung devised a technique called amplification to draw forth the meaning of a dream not only from the personal unconscious but also from the deeper collective unconscious, thus enabling the individual to connect with his or her own personal myth. Jung was convinced a person possessing a fair degree of self-understanding and psychological savvy could get to the meaning of his personal unconscious without the assistance of an expert; to understand the depths of the collective unconscious, however, required the guidance of a trained Jungian analyst.

Amplification entails elaborating and expanding upon key dream elements. It involves giving a comprehensive, detailed description of the symbol and its history. In this way, the symbol grows and often transforms, revealing its mythic aspects that belong to the collective unconscious. Though a thorough interpretation of these mythic elements requires a Jungian analyst, it's still possible to discern a great deal without one.

This exercise works well with dream images about which you have unresolved feelings and ones that make a strong impact on your senses and/or thoughts. Choose a person or an image in an important dream. Allow it to speak to you; ask it: "Who are you? What do you wish to tell me?" Describe its physical appearance and attitude, tell its background, where it came from. Examine it in relation to the "real" world, to the context of the dream, and to your personal associations. Look at all the different facets of the image. Elaborate on the image until it takes over and elaborates itself, perhaps even changing form. Go with it completely, write down everything without censoring yourself. You may be amazed by what you discover.

One of my students gained an important insight into a recurring image that pained her in both her waking and dreaming life, through this technique. Her cat, Beulah, had unexpectedly died ten months before, and her grief was still unusually fresh and overwhelming; for some reason the wound just wouldn't heal. During this time, she was in an intense period of therapy, examining the myth of perfection she had built around her mother in order to avoid confronting the reality that her mother gave her very little of what she emotionally needed. Beulah often appeared in her dreams, and the following dream was particularly painful.

Kitten

I'm showing a friend some photographs of myself that are in a yearbook or photo album. We look at a picture of me with a group of friends and my kitten Mickey; I had just gotten her the day before and she was very tiny.

Suddenly, I am in the photograph and it's a live scene. Mickey walks toward me. I remember that I have her because my beloved Beulah recently died. The kitten turns from orange to black; it's Beulah when she was a kitten. Then it becomes Mickey again as the awful, irreversible reality of Beulah's death becomes real again. I start to cry, and wake up.

The dreamer's initial interpretation of the dream was that Beulah represented her recent period of relative happiness, her first since the cat died. She felt that she was worried that no matter how hard she worked to protect and keep alive this new-found contentment, it would still be very fragile and could be yanked away from her at any time. She then wrote this amplification of Beulah.

Beulah

She is a teddy bear of a cat: soft, plump, irresistibly squeezable. She is perfect, everything I could want and everything I've ever wanted, all in one complete package. She is my baby; I take care of her and protect her. She is made to be loved by me; that is her role in life. My life is irrevocably tied to hers; she is part of me, my best part, my perfection. She is ultimate love, softness, and warmth. I belong to her. She loves me completely, without reservation or ambivalence, and always. All I have to do is love her back and she is mine forever. She is total, perfect, unconditional love. She is Mother.

Through amplifying the image of Beulah, she arrived at the collective unconscious archetype "Mother," which then led her to her personal unconscious image of her mother. She saw that she was using the death of Beulah as a way of dealing with the "death" of the myth of her mother as an all-loving person who fulfilled the requirements of the archetype "Mother." The pain of acknowledging that her mother could never satisfy her needs was too devastating for her to experience directly. Grieving over Beulah enabled her to work through the demise of her "perfect mother" myth on a level she could tolerate.

Symbols can be amplified not only in their present-day context, but they can also be carried into the past and future. These projections can further expand a symbol's dimensions, adding new possibilities for insight, as was shown when this technique was applied to the following dream:

Wildebeests

Three wildebeests charge out of the ocean; there may be others behind them. I warn the person I'm with to move quickly because although the wildebeests aren't intentionally dangerous, they are very wild and tend to kick a lot.

The other person and I drag the blanket we're lying on away from the wildebeests and the ocean. An injured bird is being dragged through the sand. I tell my mother, who apparently is the person with me, "Be careful, it's alive." She has picked it up by its feet. She still hurts it as she lifts it because she doesn't support its whole body, but she manages to perch it on a tree limb where it seems comfortable. I'm aware that my mother is afraid to touch it. I later find the bird curled up in a box which it has managed to get into by itself. But the bird still looks half-dead.

We see a man in a phone booth. His eyes are swollen. In fact, someone else is horrified by the condition of one eye, which I don't see. He's trembling.

The man has managed to escape from a car that is half-sunk in the water. With tears in my eyes, I ask him how he freed himself. He doesn't really give an answer. My emotion is not shared by the others present, including the man, and so it disappears.

In her initial reaction to the dream, the dreamer regarded wildebeests as an expression of her wild nature. However, she couldn't relate this meaning to the rest of the dream. It wasn't until she amplified the image "wildebeest" and carried it forward into the future and back into the past that she was able to understand the dream's message. Her present, future, and past amplifications of the symbol are:

Wildebeests (In the Present)

Frightening in a herd, because they are oblivious to anything that might be in their way, and will stampede and trample.
Dumb.
Amusing to look at—so ungainly.
Likable and sweet individually.
Playful.
They like to romp.
By following the herd, thousands have died by falling off cliffs.
No sense of individual survival.
Many have suffered terribly from attacks by other wild animals.
Pregnant mothers, alone and helpless, have been killed by predators.
Also known as gnus.

Wildebeests (Projected into the Future)

They are moving toward pain and death in their journey with the herd. Their destination is an unhappy one, but they don't know their survival is at risk.

Wildebeests (Projected into the Past)

The life of the wildebeests has always been this way, since their inception. Wildebeests therefore must represent ill-fated destiny. Wildebeests must be a universal archetypal symbol of strong feelings destroyed.

Before the dreamer did these symbol amplifications, "wildebeests" represented to her an untamed wildness that was out of control and therefore harmful to anything in its way. Once she did the dreamwork, however, she recognized a prophetic message in the dream: The animal part of our nature—the emotions that spring from the unconscious (the ocean)—is subject to pain, injury, and eventual death. By relating the symbol of "wildebeests" to the other symbols in the dream, she was able to arrive at a more complete understanding of it. For example, there is a repetition of the "wildebeests" meaning in the injured bird and in the man who survived the automobile accident in which he almost drowned (again, water is a symbol for feelings). His eye (I) is injured, something which the dreamer refused to see in the dream.

The indifference of the mother toward the injured bird and the lack of sympathy for the injured man can be compared to the indifference of life toward the wildebeests, who are subject to hardship and destruction; the world for them is uninterested rather than protecting.

Therefore, the symbol of the wildebeests is crucial to the understanding of the dream. In the final analysis, the dream says that an individual's life force, his animal nature, needs to be guided and protected when he is developing into an adult. If it isn't, pain and destruction will be the result. The dreamer then reflected upon the indifference she experienced in her childhood and how it had led to an attitude of hopelessness in her present life.

E X E R C I S E 1 1

Completing the Plot

Jung's work on the connection between the unconscious and the conscious, the dream life and the waking life, led him to develop another dreamwork technique called active imagination, or completing the plot. In this exercise, the dreamer rewrites the ending or completes the plot of his dream in a waking state. This exercise, which is also effective in conjunction with other dreamwork exercises, enables the dreamer to experience power in his life by creating a positive, feeling resolution to an incomplete or unsatisfactory situation. The connection between dream life and waking life is a two-way street; changes in dreams often foreshadow changes in waking life.

A patient commented that he only noticed the changes in his life after he realized that his dreams had changed. Another patient was particularly impressed with the way this dreamwork technique affected his life. He initially had very little confidence in his ability to attract women. In a dream, he meets a woman whom he likes, but she tells him she must leave. She disappears, and he wakens feeling hopeless and depressed. I suggested he use his waking imagination to meet her again and make a date with her. After writing out the scenario the way he wanted it to go, he reported that his depression disappeared and that he felt a newly earned sexual confidence.

A student had great success with this technique in the following dream, which she found profoundly disturbing.

Excluded from the Party

My friend P takes me to a party at a huge mansion, much like the one in which I grew up. He's dressed in a tuxedo. I wasn't invited to the dinner party but I've come with him and am going to wait for him in a bedroom until the party is over.

We enter the mansion, and P and a maid take me to a little bedroom on the first floor near the dining room; that's where I'm supposed to wait. P warmly says goodbye, then he and the maid leave. The door of the room is left open. I feel OK about the situation.

From the room, I can see there are a lot of guests in tuxedos and evening gowns having cocktails before dinner. I see P enjoying himself. Some people come into the bedroom and talk to me. P walks by but doesn't look in the room.

Everyone sits down for dinner. By peeking out the door I can see part of the long table where everyone is seated. Time drags on and I feel trapped and bored. My cats appear, as if brought there to amuse me while I wait, and I take care of them.

A dark young man enters the room as I'm cleaning the cat litter box; he had come in and talked to me before. He's hostile, and says something mean about P not really liking me. Using the cat litter scoop, I hurl a piece of cat shit onto his face and it sticks on his cheek. He leaves the room, furious.

I have to get out of this house without being seen. I feel great resentment toward P and the people giving the party; why wasn't I invited? My mother appears, dressed like a maid. She sneaks me into a deep, narrow closet; I recognize it as one of her own. We get to the end of the closet, but it doesn't seem like there's anything there. She tells me she can help me escape now. I desperately want to go but I worry about my cats; there are three of them back in the room, too many to carry out in my arms and I don't know where their carrying case is. I become anxiously preoccupied with the logistics of transporting them and am stuck. The dream turns lucid for a split second; I'm aware that I am dreaming and thus don't have to worry about the cats. I escape, glad to be out of the mansion.

It's the next morning in my dream. I eat breakfast with my mother, father, and sister. My sister says that she was at a party last night, and heard that I was there and had thrown cat shit on someone. I'm not surprised that she didn't come to visit me in the bedroom; she doesn't like me. My father sheepishly announces that he was at the party, too, and also knew I was trapped in the bedroom. I am enraged, screaming and crying with shock and betrayal. He cringes at my verbal assault, looking slightly embarrassed, but he's not really contrite. He casually mentions that he remembers standing on the mansion's roof garden, looking at the stars and thinking of me trapped in the bedroom below. He says that he felt a little sorry for me. When I ask him why he hadn't rescued or even visited me, he says that he just didn't feel like it.

I'm hysterical with anger and hurt and continue screaming and crying but it doesn't affect them or make me feel better. I'm overwhelmed by a sense of helplessness and frustration. I wake up in tears.

The dreamer said she awoke filled with rage over her helplessness. Her feelings of being a victim made her literally sick to her stomach, and she couldn't find a way to get rid of this anger. I suggested that she complete the dream by writing an ending that would satisfy her; the following is her resolution:

Excluded from the Party (Completing the Plot)

I stop crying and screaming at my father and am silent. He watches me cautiously, unnerved by my sudden change of mood. I feel a strong, powerful anger building up in me, very different from my previous rage. I don't want to feel like a victim, and make a conscious decision not to feel that way anymore. I feel strong, filled with conviction.

I turn to my father and firmly tell him that he did a terrible thing; he betrayed me in an unconscionable way. He is the one who is bad and should suffer, not me. I tell him that even though he did something so terrible to me, he didn't, and couldn't, destroy me. I survived by saving myself. What he lacked in desire or ability to protect me I made up for in myself, and he couldn't take that away. I didn't need him anymore.

I then acknowledged to myself that I contributed to that awful predicament by agreeing to go to the party and wait in the bedroom in the first place. I should have realized that that was a degrading thing to do and that it would make me miserable. Accepting responsibility for my own part in making myself unhappy further obliterates the feeling of being a victim.

I had allowed this situation to occur; next time I won't let it happen. I had made an error in judgment, I paid the price for my mistake and survived, and now the incident is over; I can prevent it from occurring again.

I feel calm. I've made plenty of mistakes before; one more is not a big deal. If other people, including my father, behaved badly, that's their problem. I don't have to be dependent on anyone else; I can protect myself.

Doing this exercise freed the dreamer from her feelings of helplessness. It made her even more aware of the power and control she could exert over her life, and pointed out that she could take care of herself and survive even when those who were supposed to protect her betrayed her instead. The simple act of rewriting the ending of her dream produced the insight she needed, and she was able to transform a negative dream experience into a positive one that enhanced her feelings of strength and power.

This technique is invaluable with any dream that ends in a painful or unsatisfactory manner. Learning to take control and create positive options in your dream life enhances your ability to do that in your waking life.

The connection between the conscious and unconscious, made accessible through dreamwork, offers us unlimited opportunities for growth and discovery. Jung emphasized this inherent potential when he wrote:

Whoever nurtures this contact between conscious and unconscious will, in time, experience a great spiritual and moral release of tension, his inner oppositions will be lessened; he will take root in his instinct and gain that sense of security and support which is beyond the reach of the intellect and will with its oscillating relations. At the same time there will develop in him an undreamed-of fullness of life that expands rather than shrinks with age because the instincts and values are being truly lived.[5]

7

Fritz Perls and Gestalt Therapy

What are you experiencing right now? What are your feelings, your body sensations, your facial expression, your level of tension, at this precise moment? To Fritz Perls, the father of gestalt therapy, the here and now was all-important. Unlike the psychoanalyst, the gestalt therapist is not concerned with reconstructing the past. Gestalt therapy attempts to make the patient aware of what is hiding within himself and then to take responsibility for it. Awareness is the key. The more a person can experience himself, the more he can change. Perls wrote, "When we come to our senses, we start to *see*, to *feel*, to experience our needs and satisfactions instead of playing roles and needing such a lot of props."[1] There are no intellectual explanations and interpretations here; the therapist doesn't ask *why*, but rather *what* and *how*.

Fritz Perls, like Jung, was an advocate of psychoanalysis before breaking away to start his own school. Born in 1893, he was a contemporary of Jung and Freud, though it's clear that each of these three men had his own unique approach to dreaming. Freud hoped to resolve neurosis by bringing unconscious material into awareness. Jung aimed to help the person find the archetypal images suitable in the growth toward self. Perls attempted to uncover and bring forth parts of the personality that were missing.

Perls originated some, but not all, of his conceptions. He took theories and techniques from a multitude of traditions and disciplines (among them Wilhelm Reich's philosophy of body awareness, Eastern religion, existentialism, and psychodrama), blended them together, tossed in a few ideas of his own, and created a whole. That is what a gestalt is—a whole, or totality. Gestalt therapy aims to restore the personality to its true gestalt, or wholeness, by contacting the missing parts of self, the personality functions that have been crippled.

In gestalt therapy, the patient is asked to tell his dream as if it were happening in the present, at that very instant. This is true of recent dreams as well as dreams that occurred many years before. Jung had written, "The whole dream-work is essentially subjective, and a dream is a theatre in which the dreamer is himself the scene, the player, the prompter, the producer, the author, the public, and the critic . . . all the figures in the dream [are] personified features of the dreamer's own personality."[2] Perls agreed; however, he worked differently than Jung. While Jung asked the person to amplify, to make the image larger in order to tap the feelings contained in images from the collective unconscious, Perls attempted to explode the image by having the patient express the feelings contained within the image.[3]

EXERCISE 12

Be Everything in Your Dream

Perls's method for doing this was to ask the dreamer to become every element in his dream, both animate and inanimate, and then have the elements carry on a dialogue. Elements usually start off in conflict, opposing one another. By giving full expression to each element, the person eventually arrives at a feeling resolution.[4] This means that at the very least a temporary solution is discovered for the problem, since every element of the dream is a projection of the person.[5]

This exercise works well with a dream partner; you can tape-record it if you want to transcribe it into your dream journal later. You, the dreamer, first relate the dream to your dream partner in its entirety. Then, your dream partner guides you as you retell it—directing you to be first one element and then another, instructing you when to engage in a dialogue between the different elements, etc. It's essential that your dream partner listen carefully to the dream in order to choose the optimum moments to do the exercise.

The following is an example of how a dream partner used this exercise to guide a dreamer to an understanding of the meaning of a disturbing dream.

DREAMER: A few nights ago I dreamed that I was leaving a dinner party and taking home a prepared fish that was left over from the party.

DREAM PARTNER: Tell the dream as if it's happening now.

DREAMER: The fish is extremely ugly. As I get on the elevator, a woman with a straw bag knocks the point of the bag into the fish. I pull the fish back, sensing that it's still alive. I look at the woman with annoyance but she is oblivious to me and to what she has done. I want to confront her but she won't notice me and I feel frustrated and helpless. I feel the fish moving in the plastic bag and become anxious. It's hard to believe that this fish that's been scaled and had its insides removed could still be alive. I'm filled with disgust but at the same time want to save the fish's life. I try to protect it from being bumped by other people on the elevator. The fish has become enormous and begins thrashing around. I sense that if it doesn't get into water immediately it will die. I am in a panic. The elevator stops on the ground floor. I rush out and there's an ocean. I run to the ocean, pull the plastic bag off part of the fish, and put it in the water. I expect to see the fish slowly sink to the bottom after a struggle, but instead it comes to life and bounds into the onrushing waves with great force.

DREAM PARTNER: Experience yourself as the fish in the bag, in the elevator. What does it feel like to be this fish?

DREAMER: I can't breathe. I feel dead but I want to live. I am naked and exposed. My insides hurt where they have taken out my guts. I've been scaled on the outside and feel raw. I'm ugly. I've been waiting around to be eaten, but no one wanted me. I am left over. I am humiliated. I am a fish out of water. I need to breathe or I will die. I am suffocating.

DREAM PARTNER: Have a dialogue between the fish and yourself in the dream.

DREAMER: (Fish): Let me out!

(ME): I can't let you out; you'll die. I'm trying to protect you.

(FISH): I don't want your protection, I want my freedom! Why are you doing this to me?

(ME): I don't know, I hate this. You were given to me, for lunch tomorrow. You're supposed to be dead.

(FISH): If you keep me, I will be dead. I don't want to die!

(ME): Trust me, I'll let you go when it's safe. Soon, but not now. Stop growling and just wait.

(FISH): No! If I trust you and wait, I'll die!

DREAM PARTNER: How does it feel to be the plastic bag?

DREAMER: I am strong, but not that strong. I can be ripped. I hold, I keep something inside of me, but I am transparent; I don't hide what I hold. I don't like what is inside me; it's ugly and dangerous. But my job is to contain it. I am gripped at the top by the person who is carrying me. I am in that awful position of holding something inside that I don't like, but I have no freedom of my own; I am controlled by someone else.

DREAM PARTNER: Have a dialogue between the fish and the bag.

DREAMER: (Fish): Let me out!

(BAG): I can't let you out. It's not up to me.

(FISH): Then I'll break you open!

(BAG): Why can't you lie still?! I'm protecting you from being trampled to death. If you break me open you will be destroyed, and I will be torn and empty. Stop giving me such a terrible time! I never wanted you inside me.

(FISH): If you don't let me out, I will die!

(BAG): Then you will die either way. But I don't want to be broken.

DREAM PARTNER: Now have a dialogue between the bag and yourself.

DREAMER: (Bag): Look at the position you've put me in. I don't want to hold this fish, and it doesn't want to be in me. Why don't you just set us free?

(ME): Because I can't. I'm not free, I'm a victim of this, too.

(BAG): Then who's in control here?

(ME): I don't know. Maybe no one's in control. I don't know, but I know it isn't me.

DREAM PARTNER: Be the woman who jabs the fish with her bag.

DREAMER: I am oblivious and indifferent and can overlook and ignore the person who's having the struggle with the fish. I don't care whether the fish lives or dies. I am unconcerned and preoccupied with other things.

DREAM PARTNER: Now be yourself in the dream —the person holding the fish in the plastic bag.

DREAMER: I am left holding the bag. I wish I had never decided to take this fish home. I'm horrified by it but feel responsible for it. I'm angry at that woman who jabbed it with her bag. And I feel helpless because she won't listen to me; she could jab it again. Nobody here realizes my dilemma; if the fish gets away it will slither on the floor and they will step on it. I must protect it, get it to water before it dies. I'm having a terrible time trying to hold onto it; it doesn't realize I'm trying to help. It's going to get away. It's dying and I can't let it die.

DREAM PARTNER: Be the fish when it gets into the water.

DREAMER: Now that I am in my right environment, I am powerful again and completely alive.

DREAM PARTNER: Give the dream the ending you want it to have.

DREAMER: The fish swims in the ocean; it feels free, alive, happy, and beautiful. As it swims it notices other fish like it nearby. I, as the rescuer of the fish, feel exalted. The bag has sunk to the bottom of the ocean and I don't care; it's obsolete, no longer necessary. I don't have to contain the life (symbolized by the fish) that was inside me. I don't have to protect or hold the fish anymore. Before I was both the fish and the bag. Now I am just the fish; I have rescued myself.

Through this exercise, the dreamer discerned the dream's message. She became aware of her extreme frustration at asserting herself in the face of indifference; indifference is dangerous and destructive to life. Nevertheless, even though indifference was destroying her life at the beginning of the dream, her life force became strong again and won out. She also realized that the indifference she is fighting is not just external but is within her as well; she has allowed this event to occur. The unconcerned woman with the handbag is a part of her. Through this dream she learned that she was destroying the life force within her by trying to protect it. Her life force, though, is stronger than the part protecting it and eventually wins out and is set free. Her basic desire is to live and be open despite all her past injuries, hurts, and insults.

This dream exercise contains several gestalt principles. The dreamer tells the dream in the present even though it took place a few nights before; the emphasis is always on the here and now, even with experiences from the past. The dreamer experiences all the sensations and feelings of the elements in the dream. Obviously this can take a long time so the dream partner selected the most important parts with which to work. If there had been more time, he would have asked the dreamer to be the elevator, the straw bag, the ocean, etc., and then directed her to have these elements talk to each other. The dreamer is every part of her dream, just as every person finds in life the mirror of himself. There is no analysis or interpretation in this exercise; the goal is for the dreamer to experience her own thoughts, feelings, and sensations and from that experience to understand the meaning of the dream. The dreamer must take responsibility for it, for only she can determine its validity and be responsible for her life. By continuing the dream at the end (similar to Jung's completion-of-the-plot technique), the dreamer is able to discover a new gestalt, or configuration. The dreamer said that this exercise left her with a feeling of excitement and aliveness. Through the dreamwork, she had begun to reclaim that part of herself that was being squelched—her feelings and her life force. This is what an experience of awareness can evoke, even if the insight is a painful one.

You don't have to have a dream partner to be everything in your dream; rewriting the dream as a play in your dream journal accomplishes the same thing. This format makes it easy to experience the dream in the present and provides a convenient structure for expressing the feelings of each element (through interior monologues similar to those in Shakespeare) and having them talk to each other. Your dream ego (the element in the dream that you recognize as "self") can be indicated by "I" or "Me." According to Perls, of course, all the other images are parts of you, too, but since they're not consciously recognized as such they are referred to as "projections."

In the following example, the dreamer initially wrote out the dream, then rewrote it as a play and added the ending she wanted.

The Sniper

I am going to visit a close friend on a beautiful day.

I: I am a confident person, capable and strong. I'm happy today because I'm looking forward to seeing my friend. I have been close to him for a long time.

As I'm walking, I suddenly hear what sounds like a bullet zinging at me; it just misses me. I turn just in time to see a SNIPER, a devilish-looking young woman dressed in a black turtleneck, dark jeans, and sneakers, run around the corner. Before she disappears she gives me an evil, leering grin.

SNIPER: I skulk against walls, waiting. I can appear and disappear at will, anytime, anywhere. I see my victim coming; malicious joy spurts like blood from my black heart. I lay my ears flat back against my head like the cat I am and hiss softly in anticipation. I raise my gun, aim, and fire. It is a delicious feeling, this one of destruction and power. Power not to kill but better, slower than that, the power to drive to insanity. Again and again I shoot at her; I make her dance my dance.

I am terrified of the sniper. I see she is not shooting bullets at me but rather PAPER ROCKETS, little gray cones, but that doesn't make a difference. I run around hysterically, trying to avoid them. Even though they don't hit me I seem to feel their sting.

PAPER ROCKETS: We know the true power we have. We are only made of paper, seemingly fragile, yet we can terrify like steel. We deceive and our deception is believed. There's no need for us to be more than we are; our victim will make us into something more horrid than we ourselves could create.

My terror grows. The sniper appears and disappears like the Cheshire Cat—I never know where she'll turn up next. I become frantic and confused.

   I: Stop this! Who are you?
   SNIPER: I don't have to answer your questions.
   I: There must be some mistake. Why are you doing this?
   SNIPER: There's no mistake; I chose you. But I won't tell you why.
   I: I don't deserve this!
   SNIPER: What makes you so sure of that? And why should I care? I don't care.

I continue to hysterically run around in circles, trying to elude the paper rockets. The sniper laughs and laughs. I finally arrive at my FRIEND's house and pound on his door until he opens it. He is wearing a cheery red ski sweater, his blond hair is cut short, and his eyes are a brighter blue than usual.

   FRIEND: I love my dear friend. We have known each other a long time and have been through many things together. I love myself even more and am very sure of myself. My perceptions are usually correct.

I desperately try to explain to my friend about the sniper and the paper rockets, but it seems that he can't see them.

I: Help me, please help me! Protect me! She's going to kill me!

FRIEND: Who's going to kill you? There's no one there.

I: *She* is, the sniper. Look—there! And there!

FRIEND: What are you talking about? There's *no one* there. Calm down!

I: I can't calm down! Don't you see the paper rockets?

FRIEND: What paper rockets? Why would you be afraid of paper rockets anyway?

I: They can kill me, or worse. Please believe me! I need you to believe me!

FRIEND: You're acting crazy, not like yourself. I can't help you if you're not you.

I: (to sniper): Why can't he see you? Aren't you real?

SNIPER: Oh, yes, I'm real. You *know* I'm real. But I want you to be alone. The more you ask for help, the more alone you will be, because he will doubt your sanity. You will lose your credibility. He will leave you even though he loves you, even though you need him now more than ever. When you are alone there will be no validation, no corroboration. You will slowly dissolve, evaporate into nothingness, and yet retain just enough awareness to know that you are nothingness.

I continue trying to convince my friend that I am in danger, and I alienate him in the process.

FRIEND: I have to leave you. I can't help you. I try, I do all I can, but it's not enough and there's no more I can do. I don't understand you and you frighten me. You are definitely not you; I don't know who you are. I know there is no sniper, I know you are safe, but I can't convince you. I love you but I must leave. Come back when you are again the B I know.

He leaves and I am alone again with the smirking sniper.

SNIPER: See, I was right. We are always right, my paper rockets and me. You are alone and you will always be alone because I will always be here. You will never again be the person you once were. You are all mine, and no one hates you the way I do.

The sniper continues to shoot paper rockets at me.

The Sniper (Rewriting the Ending)

Instead of running from the paper rockets, I chase after them. I catch them in my hands and crush them, tear them to pieces, set them on fire and watch them burn. I *know* them for the harmless paper they are and am no longer afraid of them. Then I turn on the sniper. She is nervous now that she sees her paper rockets have lost their power. She can't hide behind them anymore and she has no other weapons. I run after her and grab her; as soon as I touch her she vanishes. She reappears someplace else but her image is fainter. She doesn't frighten me anymore; I know that I have substance and am real, and she is not. Every time I reach out and grab her she disappears, and she is fainter every time she reappears, like a fading image, until she disappears completely. I feel powerful and effective, even stronger than before. I go see my friend. He apologizes for not listening to me. He tells me he will never leave me again, no matter how different I seem. I am glad he apologizes and we feel close to each other again.

At the time B had this dream, she was in a period of great change in her life; she was giving up a stable job in order to pursue the riskier career of a free-lance writer. B always prided herself on being strong, confident, and competent, and disdained any signs of weakness. Initially elated by the decision she had made, she was feeling depressed at the time of this dream, and didn't know why.

Through writing this dream as a play and becoming the different parts, she realized that the paper rockets were her doubts about her talent and this career change, and the sniper was her fear and self-loathing at doubting herself. In her waking life she was like her friend in the dream—unable to acknowledge these feelings because there was no place for them in her strong image of herself. Acknowledging these emotions would destroy that image and leave her weak, helpless and ineffectual. Through this dream she saw that this denial had made her fear of self-doubt enormously powerful and had put her in a precarious position. It was clear that this fear was incapacitating her, and that there was no way her current "confidence" or "strength" could help her deal with it. Instead of running from these feelings, she had to accept them and confront them head-on.

In completing the plot she brings forth the missing parts of her personality and thus creates a new gestalt, or wholeness of self. She reaches out and grabs these doubts instead of trying to escape them, and in doing so finally feels them as controllable and harmless. Once she acknowledges that feelings of self-doubt aren't so terrible, she can then confront and destroy her fear and shame of those feelings. She still retains her self-confidence by renewing her relationship with her friend, but that self-confidence is altered (via the apology) and can now include these newly discovered facets of herself. The dreamwork thus gave her an insight about herself that she is now trying to incorporate into her life.

It's not necessary to be a professional or even amateur writer to do this exercise—the goal is not a Broadway play but rather a discovery of hidden aspects of yourself. The theatrical format is only used as a means to facilitate this discovery. To rewrite your dream as a play, write an introductory monologue for each new element as you present it. You become that part as you have it define itself and its feelings in the first-person form. When two elements conflict in the story, carry out a dialogue between them. Alternate your point of view between them until each has spoken its piece. Then continue with the story until the next element or point of conflict is reached. Write freely and spontaneously; the aim is not to make it "good" in a literary sense but rather to seize hold of any emotions that come to the surface. Rewrite the ending of the dream so that it satisfies your needs and desires. You may be surprised by the elements of yourself that emerge, but it's only by accepting all the components of yourself, even those parts that make you uncomfortable, that you will feel truly whole.

8

Discoveries from the Senoi

Paradise Lost

I magine a harmonious, peaceful society, free from violent crime and mental and physical illness, whose fundamental tenet is "Cooperate with your fellows—if you must oppose their wishes, oppose them with goodwill."[1] Sound too good to be true? Well, this society actually existed, prior to World War II. How did the people accomplish this? For one thing, their culture was primarily based on a highly sophisticated understanding and use of dreams.

The Senoi (meaning "one of us") are aboriginals who live in the mountainous jungles of Malaysia. It is not known when their dream culture began, but it arouses awe and humility when we recognize how psychologically advanced these so-called primitive people were. According to Freud and his followers, repressed feelings are at the root of mental disturbance. And in our modern

society, years and years of training are required to treat
the psychologically disturbed. The Senoi, however, had
an approach to living that left no room for neurosis.
They supported and encouraged the creative fulfillment
of every member of their society. They never allowed
repressions to develop because they immediately released their emotions in their dreams. From early childhood, the Senoi were trained never to run away from
their dream feelings—be they terror or pleasure, both of
which can be equally threatening. This took great courage because feelings can be as powerful in the dream
state as they are in the waking state. The Senoi truly
accepted all emotion. However, they also understood
that total abandonment to feelings could lead to chaos,
so they chose to express them safely, though still retain-
ing all their intensity and ramifications, in their dreams.
It is a brilliant solution to the dilemma that has troubled
mankind since its inception—the handling of emotion.
We have much to learn from the Senoi.

Although the Senoi people still exist today, they under-
went a drastic change after World War II when Com-
munist terrorists invaded their territory, made them
relocate, and forced them to participate in acts of vio-
lence that led to what they referred to as "blood drunk-
enness."[2] Their great courage made them extraordinary
warriors. Afterwards, the Senoi attempted to reestablish
their tribal, nonviolent, dream-based life-style, but the
introduction of money for crops diminished their need to
share with one another. This, together with the previous
trauma they suffered, prevented them from returning to
their old culture.[3]

Most of the information about the Senoi in this
chapter comes from the work of the American psycholo-

gist and anthropologist Kilton Stewart and the British anthropologist Herbert Noone. They spent several years in Malaysia studying the prewar Senoi, and their research and writings provide the bulk of knowledge available about this culture. Anthropologists and psychologists alike have studied their findings, attempting to discover how this one group of people was able to achieve the seemingly impossible dream: a society that provides a contented, creative, fulfilling life for every member of the community.[4]

The dream philosophy of the Senoi seems more sophisticated, in practice, than any other created so far. Their method of using their dreams to effect change, growth, good fellowship, and cooperation in their lives is truly inspiring. I can't resist speculating that their development and utilization of their right-brain functions was partially responsible for their high quality of life. The Senoi and other so-called "primitive" cultures live more by their intuition, feelings, and imagination (right-brain functions) than by reason and logic (left-brain functions). This was especially true in the Senoi society with its heavy reliance on dreams. This does not mean that reason and logic didn't play a part in their way of thinking, but rather that they didn't inhibit or take precedence over the right-brain functions. Perhaps the Senoi achieved the optimum balance in the use of both sides of their brains.

Though the Senoi themselves have lost their dream culture, we can use many of their dream principles to enrich and empower our own lives.

The Senoi believed their dream world was connected to the spirit world; thus every dream was important since it might be a message from a supernatural force. The philosophy behind their dream approach was that every person had ultimate power over evil as long as he had the cooperation of other tribe members and the courage to use that inherent power. Through his dream bravery, an individual could free the souls from his body. Once these souls were free, they could move about and come to his aid when he needed them. Fear made the souls retreat into the body, where they became paralyzed. In our culture, these souls can be compared to the repressed self-destructive energy that prevents us from reaching our full potential.

EXERCISE 13

Fight to the End—From Victim to Victor

Since courage is the chief weapon against evil, the Senoi were taught to fight danger, not retreat from it. If a Senoi child dreamed of a monster coming after him, he did not run away and hide. Rather, he attacked the monster and fought to the end. Simply by following parental instruction, all Senoi children were able to master their dream fears by the time they reached adolescence. The child's parents had taught the child that he or she, in fact, had nothing to fear, nothing to lose. If, by some chance, the child died in the dream, it meant that he or she had reduced some of the opponent's strength, and the child would immediately be reborn into a better body.

The odds were, however, that the dreamer would kill the dream enemy. The opponent's death released a positive force from the part of the dreamer that created the destructive force. This positive force would become a dream friend whose support the dreamer could enlist in times of trouble. Like Freud, Jung, and Perls, the Senoi were aware that dreams expressed various aspects of the dreamer. According to Kilton Stewart, as the Senoi destroyed his enemies in his dreams, he overcame the destructive parts of himself and freed that energy for creativity.

Fighting our dream dangers to the end can give us the same psychological benefits that doing so gave the Senoi. It is the ideal way to work with nightmares. Simply by telling yourself that you must fight your dream enemies rather than run away from them—just as the Senoi parents told their children—you may discover that you can succeed in defeating your dream foe. Some dreamers report instant success; others require more time for the idea to sink in. Telling yourself that you will fight to the end is the first step. A second step is to rewrite your frightening dreams in your waking state, with the intent of destroying your dream enemies instead of running away. Creating your tormentor's death scene can provide a cathartic release as you transform yourself from victim to victor.

This dream was a recurring nightmare until the dreamer envisioned herself destroying her torturers.

The Torturers

Teenage hoodlums capture me and take me to my parent's house. The house then changes and becomes a kind of concentration camp. Two short men hold me captive. My left breast is exposed and they are cutting it. There is no pain or blood; it's as if I've been given a local anesthetic there. They have a razor very close to my nipple but they don't cut. Yet somehow they succeed in detaching my nipple from my breast. Then, it's as if I'm flat-chested with my nipple separated and a ring through it. During this, the two men are smiling. Their message seems to be "We will be pleasant if you obey." I become filled with hate. I can feel my eyes gleaming. I know I'm leading myself into more danger, but my hatred and outrage are so strong that I can't let them get away with it. I hit one of them, and their friendliness disappears in-stantly. They drag me down a long corridor, toward a room where I know I will be tortured. I wake up.

In writing out the dream, the dreamer successfully battled these men.

The Torturers—Fight to the End

I decide I would rather die than allow myself to be tortured by these men, and therefore make up my mind to fight them to the death. I manage to pull away from them and am tempted to run, but in-stead resolve to stick to my original plan to kill them. I become a mass of energy, like a whirling dervish, arms and legs flailing about in a frenzied way. I seem to have more than just two arms and two legs, and they move so fast you can't see them. My long hair flies wildly around and I can't really see through it. I can't see or feel the two men as I strike out; all my senses are overwhelmed by this incredible, tornado-like energy. I finally stop what I'm doing to survey the situation. The men have disappeared and the corridor looks different, nonthreatening. I know that I have permanently destroyed the men; it's as if my energy was so strong that I not only killed them; I made them evaporate as well.

The ultimate objective, however, is to learn to fight to the end while you are dreaming. Doing the writing exercise just mentioned will help inculcate this intention in your mind. Also, remind yourself as you fall asleep that you want to fight your dream enemies, not run away or wake up.

EXERCISE 14

Demand Gifts from Your Dream Enemies

The Senoi were taught not just to fight their dream foes but also to demand gifts from them. When the danger was inanimate, such as fire or smoke, the Senoi entered into the danger and found a gift. The gift could be anything from a poem, story, or painting to the answer to a problem, an invention, or a new skill.

You can also receive valuable experiences and insights by demanding gifts from your dream enemies, and thus get the maximum potential benefits from your dream. You can implant this idea in your mind by regularly requesting gifts from dream characters in all your written dreamwork. As you're falling asleep at night, tell yourself that you want to get gifts in your dreams.

This dreamer wrote out forceful, positive resolutions for several of her nightmares, always making sure that she received something of value from her dream enemies. This positive thinking carried over into her dream state, and eventually she was able both to fight her enemies and demand gifts from them while she was having the dream. The following is an example of how she utilized these skills.

Horror Movie Dream

I am with a busload of people, following another busload of people, on a highway at night. It is some sort of social outing. We are driving through the mountains, with rocks and boulders on either side of us, and we encounter a lot of ground fog. As we round a curve, the first bus goes out of control and hurtles down the cliffside.

We all pile out of our bus and run to the edge of the cliff and look down. All the people on the other bus are dead; we can see all these broken, twisted bodies among the rocks. We're all traumatized, horrified and terrified. Someone goes down the cliff and verifies that everyone is dead. He comes back up and we talk about how we have to go for help.

Suddenly there is movement in one of the bodies. It gets up and starts climbing up the hill toward us. It has a completely ghostlike face and vacant, staring eyes. I think, "Oh God, it's the un-dead!" We're all mesmerized, rooted to the spot with fear. Then a second body starts coming up the cliff, and a third and a fourth. We realize that they're coming up the hill to claim us. We're terrified and start rolling huge rocks down the hill to stop them. They simply swat the rocks away as if they are beach balls.

We are beside ourselves with fear and race back to the bus. We pile into the bus and finally the driver gets in. We have trouble closing the doors, but finally the driver gets them shut and gets the bus going, and we lurch off into the wilderness. The driver drives the bus off the road. We look out the rear window of the bus to see if the undead are coming after us, and sure enough they are running after us, pursuing us. We're very frightened and keep yelling to the bus driver, "Go faster, go faster!"

Suddenly the driver drives down into this gully, and it becomes a marshy bog. The fog is swirling all over the place and there are huge trees around us. We keep shouting to the driver, "No, no, don't go down there, we'll get stuck!" and sure enough we start getting mired in the bog. Then we see what looks like a tremendous stockade fence, and we think we're going through the gates. We drive through the gates and then the driver turns around. He has the same visage as the undead. We realize that we're trapped and they are coming for us.

The bus doors open and we scramble out of the bus and look for a way out. We see that we're in a ravine that is totally walled in; there is no way out. There are all these vague, menacing instruments of torture hanging from the stockade walls. Everyone is hysterical with fear and running wildly around. They try to climb up the sides of the ravine to get to the stockade wall, but they all slip in the mud and slide back down. Then the undead bodies start coming through the gate.

I start trying to fly; I think there must be a way out of here if I can just get up high enough. I start flying around at what seems to be tree-top or roof-top level. I'm in a total panic as I search for a way out. There doesn't seem to be any way of escape; somehow even the top seems walled in and impenetrable. It's clear I can't run away from this; my only chance for survival is to fight the undead.

I fly to the stockade wall, to the torture instruments. I see something like a razor-edged whip; somehow I know that it can dismember people. I pull it off the wall and go back down to the ravine. People are lying in the mud, moaning as they die.

The undead are killing them, but I'm not sure how.

I start flogging the undead with the whip. It cuts cleanly through them, like an egg slicer. There is no blood and they are still alive, but the pieces of their bodies separate. By severing their limbs and heads from their torsos, I can render them harmless. There are many of them and sometimes, in my haste, I forget to remove both arms or both legs, and the body comes chasing after me. My heart is pounding and sweat pours down my face, but I continue whipping the undead.

Finally they are all sliced apart; fragments of their bodies are scattered all over the ravine. Their limbs and torsos don't seem human because they're stark white and bloodless; it looks like they're made of hardboiled egg whites. The undead are still alive, though. I get the feeling that if any of the limbs get too close to a torso it can jump back on and start moving about collecting other parts until it is whole again. The body parts are all twitching and I walk around making sure none get too close together.

Then I locate what I know to be the leader of the undead. His body is all in one piece but it's clear, like raw egg white. I'm not afraid of him; I'm the victor. I feel powerful, confident, in control; it gives me an unusual sense of calm. He doesn't look frightening; he looks as if he's in his sixties, with longish, unkempt white hair and a surprisingly sweet smile. He kind of looks like a Classics professor. I forget that I was ever afraid.

I tell him, "I want a gift." He asks me what I want. I arrogantly reply, "The most valuable thing you have." It's clear I really mean it. A beautiful, brightly colored bird, that looks somewhat like a peacock, appears. Its colors seem even more vivid in comparison to the mud and gloomy dark colors in the ravine. The colors form a pattern of black, red, gold, green, and blue rectangles. The bird is magical, from another dimension, as if it just stepped off the pages of some Renaissance illuminated manuscript. It walks over to me and I look into its luminous eyes and know I have received something truly wondrous and valuable. Everything around me disappears; all that exists is me and this bird.

The dreamer reported that she awoke from this dream feeling great exhilaration; the sense of triumph and accomplishment was still with her. The whole experience seemed enormously significant; it was as if she really had killed a horde of the undead. The appearance of the bird was indeed a tremendous gift; she felt lucky to have had such a stunning visual experience. It was hard for her to believe that her own imagination had created something so incredibly glorious.

EXERCISE 15

Make Your Dream End Happily

The Senoi learned to create a happy ending for their dreams always. Bringing this about often involved a type of dreaming referred to by some writers as "power dreaming," in which they could do the impossible. Thus, if a child dreamed of falling, his parents coached him to change the falling into flying, or to dream of landing in an interesting place and finding a gift. If the child felt that this dream place offered something valuable for the rest of the community, he was urged to remember the details so that he could share them when he awoke. If the Senoi dreamer thought he was drowning, he would suddenly be able to breathe underwater. If he died in his dream, he would be instantly reborn.

You can do the same thing; just repeat to yourself that your dream will end happily. It's easy to see how training yourself to have your dreams end happily could be a tremendous psychological boost in your waking life. Vow to achieve your dream goals and fully complete your dream experiences. Every dream is different from every other dream, so the means to achieving the optimum resolution will vary; what's important is that you feel satisfied with the outcome of your dream adventure.

Here's an example of a falling dream turned by a child into an enjoyable outing.

The Plane Falls Down

It's night and I'm in a tiny plane, way up in the sky. I'm flying amid all these buildings and I'm a little frightened at times. Suddenly the tiny plane starts to slowly fall from the sky. I'm scared, but tell myself that the plane has to land someplace nice.

The plane falls into about four feet of beautiful turquoise water. There's a big tortoise in the water and it looks quite content. Then I'm out of the plane and in the water, which is warm and soothing. I pet the tortoise and have a good time.

Make love in your dream

Not only did the Senoi embrace fear in their dreams, they also embraced love. There is a valuable lesson to be learned in this: Embrace *all* your feelings, don't run away from them. When the Senoi had pleasurable, sexual dreams, they were taught to move toward the loving objects and to enjoy them to the fullest; they were encouraged to have orgasms in their dreams. It didn't matter who or what the loving object was; it could be a relative, a friend's spouse, an animal, or an inanimate object. The Senoi believed that all dream images were parts of the self and needed to be integrated and loved. After reaching orgasm, the dreamer would ask the dream lover for a gift.

You can also allow yourself to enjoy fully your sexual dreams. Don't censor yourself in terms of who your dream lovers are or how many of them you have. There's no such thing as incest or promiscuity in dreams, for your dream lovers are all just different facets of yourself appearing in erotic forms, according to Senoi doctrine.

This dreamer made love in his dream with a television personality he had long admired, and said it was the best dream he had ever had.

Making Love with S. H.

I am in the newsroom of my favorite TV news show. There I meet S. H., whom I've always been attracted to. We talk and instantly hit it off; she's even more charming and witty than I imagined.

We make plans to go out together after the evening's broadcast, and I stand in the studio and watch her work. She smiles at me during the commercial breaks and I love it. I think the cameramen and other crew members notice.

After the broadcast, we leave the studio together and go someplace wonderful. I'm not sure where or what it is, but it's cozy, romantic, and dimly lit. There's plenty of food and champagne but no waiters or other customers. We stay up very late, till dawn, talking about all kinds of important, intimate things. It's probably the best conversation I've ever had, and I think she feels the same way, too. We laugh a lot and feel very close.

In the morning we are taken by limousine to an apartment. I'm not sure whose apartment it is, mine or hers. On the way to the apartment I realize that we're in New York, because we pause next to the Brooklyn Bridge and look across the river to Manhattan. It's all so perfect, I'm so handsome and she's so beautiful that it seems like an advertisement for perfume or something.

When we get to the apartment, we make love. It's fantastic—the excitement and hunger of new lovers without any of the shyness or awkwardness. We instinctively know how to please each other. It's the best sex either of us has ever had. We make love over and over, never seeming to get tired.

Suddenly we realize that it's one minute before five P.M., the time of her news broadcast. She hasn't even called the studio to tell them that she's not coming in. She feels guilty for a moment and I feel anxious, but then she says that it's OK. They will have figured out that she's not coming in and will replace her for the night. She says she's never done anything like this before; her work has always been the most important thing to her and she could never imagine letting a personal involvement get in the way of it. But then, she had never met me. We lie in bed together, in the darkened bedroom, and watch the newscast. We laugh at the excuse they make at the beginning of the show as to why she's not there. We make love while watching the show and giggle together like children. It's terrific, the most fun I've ever had. Somehow I know that everyone in the studio realizes that she's not at work because she's with me. I envision them re-membering seeing me watch the show the day before from the studio floor while she smiled at me, and then seeing us leave together. I know they're all smiling to themselves and wondering what kind of guy I am that I can get a dedicated professional like S. H. to be so irresponsible as to miss a day's work and not even call. I'm amused by the whole thing, and kind of proud, too. I feel good about myself. I decide to go all the way, and ask her for a gift. She tells me my gift is that I will be able to call up these feelings anytime I want.

The dreamer reports that he did indeed receive that gift. Every evening when he watches the news he sees her and gets a strong rush of pleasure and well-being.

When the next dreamer became sexually excited during a frightening dream, she concentrated on the pleasurable sensations and all her fear disappeared.

The Gorilla

I'm facing a gorilla who is seated in a dentist's chair. I maintain control over the gorilla with words; he's my captive. Then the gorilla gets excited, and opens up his mouth and turns into something terrifying. I'm very frightened.

I manage to still control the gorilla; I assume it's by talking but I don't know what I say. I'm afraid, but then I get sexually excited. I have no physical contact with the gorilla, but the sexual sensations build in intensity until I'm overwhelmed by them. I'm no longer afraid, or even really aware of the gorilla. I just go with these fabulous sexual feelings until I explode in an orgasm.

The Senoi believed in letting go in their dreams: fully experiencing pleasure and fighting their enemies to the death, even when it was their own death. This form of

total release freed them from the kinds of repressions
and fears prevalent in Western society.

Senoi dream life

A key aspect of Senoi dreaming was the sharing of
dreams among the entire community. From the time a
child could talk, he or she related dreams every morning
at breakfast. The entire family—parents, grandparents,
brothers, and sisters—commended the child for having
the dream. They pointed out what the child did wrong in
it and praised the child for what he or she did right. They
instructed the child to change incorrect dream behavior
in both dream and waking life, and always encouraged
full expression of feelings in all dream encounters.

The parents also attempted to correct their mistakes
that came out in the child's dream. For example, if a
young girl had a dream in which her mother paid attention to her brother but ignored her, her mother would
hear the dream, reassure the child that she wasn't intentionally neglected, and would be careful not to do it
again. Also, both her parents would instruct her to confront her dream mother and demand what she wanted
from her. In this way, she didn't harbor unexpressed
anger toward her waking mother.[5]

After the parents listened to the child's dream, they
would trace it back to pertinent or important events of
the day before. By adolescence, Senoi children were free
of nightmares and close to assuming adult roles in the
community.

Children were not the only ones who shared their
dreams at breakfast; every member of the family would
tell a dream. Then the men, adolescent boys, and some

women would go to the village council to discuss their dreams. All dreams were respected and all dreamers were considered equals.

When the Senoi adults brought their dreams to the council, they discussed the meanings of all the dream symbols and situations. Each council member offered an interpretation, and all those who agreed on the meaning adopted the dream as a group project. When an adult related an important dream, he then led the group through a dream dance. Dream dances were performed in a trancelike state; through them, the group members were able to feel what the dreamer experienced during the dream.

The Senoi merged their dream lives with their waking ones. For instance, if a man had been hostile toward an acquaintance in a dream, he would go out of his way to be friendly to this person in his waking life. If he dreamed that someone harmed him, he would tell the dream culprit in waking life so that this person could repair his dream image. If he dreamed of someone else being hurt, he would warn that person and try to kill the harmful agent in his future dreams.[6]

Most of the Senoi's daytime activities were offshoots of these council meetings; they might make costumes and sing songs as well as perform dream dances. Adults assisted children in producing the creations that appeared in their dreams, such as poems, songs, and paintings. These communal activities unified the tribe and encouraged individual creativity and growth. They took place in the long community house, which was bordered by small cottages of family units. The Senoi could spend most of their time in dream activities because they spent a minimal amount of time on the necessities of life.

It took the community (ranging in size from fifty to

two hundred people) about a week to build a house that would last for five years. They spent about two weeks a year clearing their land for planting, and only two hours a day gathering the communal food.[7]

Although our present world and technology do not make it feasible to live the once-idyllic life of the Senoi, one group of people attempted to form a community fashioned after the Senoi. This Los Angeles-based community,[8] having as many as three hundred members, set up a similar housing arrangement—with family structures surrounding a large living-dining-cooking communal room reminiscent of the Senoi's long community house—and shared their dreams. The goal of the community was the transformation of its members through total expression of feeling in both waking life and dream life; they believed that this transformation was impossible without the support of the community.

Unfortunately, the idyllic Senoi dream culture will probably never thrive again in its original form. However, we can incorporate their dream principles into our lives and dreams, and perhaps in that way get a glimpse at how potentially satisfying and fulfilling life can be.

9

Acting Out Your Dream: The Iroquois Indians

Iroquois indians: dream forefathers of Freud

Contrary to popular belief (and probably his own), Freud was not the first person to conceive of dreams as camouflaged expressions of hidden desires and to use free association to uncover those messages. Back in the seventeenth century, the Iroquois Indians had incorporated those ideas into the very fabric of their culture. Their two frames of reference, of course, are vastly different, but the similarities in the approaches of Freud and the Iroquois are uncanny. For instance, Freud believed that the unconscious consisted of repressed wishes that appeared in disguised forms in dreams. The Iroquois asserted that the soul had innate hidden desires that could be revealed only through dreams. If those desires (which they called *Ondinnonk*) weren't satisfied, the soul would wreak its revenge by punishing the physical body through disease or death. Notice how closely this resembles the explanation psychoanalysis gives for psychosomatic illnesses! Like Freud, who distinguished between the manifest dream (the remembered dream story) and the latent dream (the dream's real message, masked in symbols), the Iroquois also believed that the dream's meaning was hidden in its images. Two centuries before Freud, the Iroquois were using free association to decipher the dream's intention. If the dreamer was unable to interpret his dream by himself, a clairvoyant was brought in to assist.[1]

Once the dream was interpreted, however, Freud and the Iroquois drastically parted company on how to use the dream to benefit the dreamer. Freud and his followers used dream interpretation to help patients understand themselves better. The Iroquois believed the way to alleviate physical and psychic distress was to gratify the soul's desire by acting out the dream, literally or symbolically. Imagine a law-abiding bank officer going on a sex rampage with his personnel and customers because he'd had a dream about that the night before! He'd be hauled off to jail or a mental hospital if he wasn't killed first. In the Iroquois society, however, it would have been perfectly permissible under certain circumstances for a respectable Iroquois to have a wild orgy with members of his tribe if his dream so dictated.[2]

It's essential to understand the radically different perspective from which the Iroquois perceived dreams. To many of us, dreams are puzzling, personal, nocturnal stories, shared with close friends when especially bizarre but not usually of great import in our external lives. But the dream, to the Iroquois, was the god, whose wishes were to be obeyed immediately. The dream, in this context of a religion, was a public affair; often an entire community would participate in fulfilling the desires of the dreamer's dream.

EXERCISE 16
Make Your Dream Come True

Though literally acting out many of our dreams today could have disastrous results, outwardly expressing the wishes of certain dreams can be highly constructive. It's imperative, of course, to use common sense and discretion in selecting dreams to be enacted, but there are some that lend themselves to this form of dreamwork.

A dream that offers a solution to a problem is obviously a good one to make come true. There is a published report of Professor Dean Nimmer, of the Massachusetts College of Art, about enacting a dream of his that prevented the college, the only state-supported independent art school in the country, from losing its funding and autonomy. In an effort to reduce spending, the Massachusetts state legislature had been considering merging the Massachusetts College of Art with the University of Massachusetts in Boston. This is the report of Professor Nimmer's dream and the result:

"'In the dream I saw a whole group of students in a politician's office drawing his portrait. . . . He was statue-like, and the rhythm and motion of students drawing were all around him.' When he awoke, Nimmer realized he had created a strategy for raising art awareness in local legislators. He wrote to each, offering student-drawn portraits. Fifty lawmakers accepted. So the students did watercolors, photographs, and drawings of the legislators—and talked about their love of art and art school. One lawmaker was heard to say, 'I can't come to the phone now; I'm being sketched.'" Nimmer's strategy worked and the school's budget was reinstated.[3]

Here's another type of dream to make come true: one in which an inhibiting block is overcome. The following dream inspired the dreamer to act it out.

I Can Ride a Bicycle

I am in a beautiful, wooded area of Germany, with a lovely bicycle path running through it. I find a bicycle and decide to ride it through the forest. Everyone tells me not to do this because I don't know how to ride a bicycle, but I insist on doing it anyway. I hop on the bike and start riding; I'm amazed at how easy it is. I ride along the path and the woods around me are beautiful. I have a great time.

In real life, the dreamer had never learned to ride a bicycle because her parents had been overprotective; they had prevented her from doing many things as a child because they were afraid she would hurt herself. There was always an implicit assumption that she would fail at anything she tried. She had this dream a few months before the alimony from her divorce ended; she was embarking on a new career and preparing to support herself for the first time in her life. Having been raised to believe that she could never do this, she was understandably nervous about this transition and worried that she might fail.

When she awoke from the dream, she instantly recognized that the bicycling represented all the instilled assumptions about what she was incapable of doing. The dream's German location immediately brought to mind her mother, a Polish woman with a heavy accent. The dreamer had always wanted to ride a bicycle and felt embarrassed that she couldn't. She decided to confront her current fears by overcoming this symbolic one: she would learn to ride a bicycle. She enlisted a sympathetic and patient friend with a bike and headed for an empty parking lot. Learning to ride a bicycle at thirty-three is harder than it is at eight, and it's harder than it was in her dream. But she was delighted to discover that it wasn't impossible; a few hours and scrapes later she was pedaling around without expecting a major disaster. She reported being surprised by her exhilarated sense of accomplishment, and realized that part of her had expected she would fail. Overcoming this block gave her renewed confidence in tackling all the other things she'd been told she couldn't do.

Of course, satisfying even the soul's most beneficent wishes is not always as simple as instantly jumping up and doing it. Using other dreamwork exercises first can enable you to gain the insights needed to enact the dream successfully. The following is an example of how I used dreamwork to enact my dream eventually.

When first teaching my course on dreams, I became aware that I was relying too much on my notes. A close friend visited my class and told me she felt much more interested in the material and me when I spoke spontaneously. Her feelings corroborated my own sense that I was hiding behind 3″ × 5″ cards, and it disturbed me.

Then I dreamed that I was speaking to my class without notes, and I awakened feeling happy and triumphant. My wish, however, couldn't be literally enacted that easily because I knew, despite my dream, that something was preventing me from speaking spontaneously. All I knew about this fear was that it was directly related to standing in front of a group of people and speaking. Unable to pinpoint the feeling, I decided to converse in writing with my class. As soon as I started to write this, I grew anxious.

To My Class

I see you as a single, huge mass out there, without individuality or separate lives. You stare at me. When I read my notes it helps me pretend that you're not there, but I keep becoming aware of you. Then I get this sick feeling that I have no reason to be up here talking. My notes don't always seem to make sense as I stand up here and read them, but at least it keeps me going and gives me a reason for being here. I feel a pain in my chest that doesn't come to the surface.

I remember something that happened when I was ten years old. My mother had come to visit me at summer camp. Some of my friends asked me to play the piano but I didn't want to. My mother gave me hard looks, as if to say "Play the piano or else!" and I felt terribly resistant. Since I wouldn't play the piano, I felt I had to do something else to placate my mother. I decided to sing (something that would drive anyone away); and I chose a song about not being able to do something that was being asked of me. While I sang, my two friends Bobby and Suzy looked at me with embarrassed grins. I enjoyed the fact that even though I was performing terribly I was loved in spite of it. When I finished my song, to the giggling of my friends, I looked over at my mother; she was not smiling.

She told me in no uncertain terms that what I had done was "simply awful"; I remember her exact words and tone of voice to this very day. I was inconsolable for the rest of that day and the next day, too.

I read you my notes to avoid this feeling of being awful. At least when I read my notes, I'm giving you interesting information, and maybe you won't notice me. If I don't use my notes I'll stumble and stutter and you'll see how vulnerable and lacking in confidence I am in front of you. But which is better: to reach some of you in a faltering way, or to seem professional and distant to all of you?

The last question to my class forced me to ask another question. I had another choice to make, one far more important than how to teach my class. I had to decide whether to continue to protect myself from something that no longer existed, or whether to communicate with people openly and directly. In choosing the latter, I saw I had to live my dream and not use my notes. I did this in my following class and was thrilled to see that I had everyone's interest. I saw that this kind of communication made my students feel freer about sharing their own feelings and experiences. The class participated more, and was the liveliest, best class I had had. The biggest bonus from this was my enhanced self-confidence.

E X E R C I S E   1 7

Acting Out Your Dream in a Group

Another way to have a powerful waking-life experience of your dream is to act it out with members of a dream group. Again, good judgment must guide you in which dreams to use; clearly you want to avoid dreams that are potentially destructive to you or another person.

The dreamer first tells the group the dream in its entirety. A dream without a cast of thousands is preferable. The group can then ask any clarifying questions about the dream and its characters. After that, the dreamer assigns each group member a role in the dream as a character or other important element, and the dream is enacted with the dreamer playing himself. The dreamer thus has the opportunity to have dialogues with the dream characters and to change the ending if he so desires.

After the dream has been enacted, the members can share the feelings they had as the characters in the dream, giving the dreamer a new perspective on his dream. He should also be encouraged to express his own feelings about the exercise: for example, the ways in which the real-life experience differed from the dream experience, the new feelings elicited, the way he feels about himself and the dream now.

A dream group selected the following dream to act out:

Fighting with My Mother

I'm in my childhood house, fighting with my mother. We hate each other and are ready to destroy each other. I say that we need to get help before we kill each other. I notice the door to the basement is open. It was locked, but now it won't close. A man is trying to get into the house through that door; he looks like a derelict. I keep hitting him over the head again and again until he is unconscious; it seems to take forever. My mother refuses to help me. I want to call the police. I go to a phone booth but a woman gets there ahead of me. I try to ask her to let me use the phone; I tell her there's an emergency, there's an intruder in my house. She isn't interested and won't give me the phone. I go to another telephone booth and try to call the police, but the phone doesn't work. I'm screaming and crying in frustration, and wake up.

The dreamer, Sally, took the role of herself in the dream. And the other group members played the mother, the man who looked like a derelict, the woman at the phone booth, and the telephone that wouldn't work. It's important not to omit key inanimate objects when acting out dreams; they, too, represent facets of ourselves that need to be understood. The following is a transcript of the enactment of the dream:

Fighting with My Mother (Enactment)

MOTHER: Sally, have you been wearing my sweaters again?

SALLY: No, mother. I'm not even your size. You're always saying that. . . .

MOTHER: Then why are they all wrinkled? Stupid little bitch, lying to me, not even covering your tracks, and then playing the little innocent. And your father thinks you're such a damn goody-goody.

SALLY: You're jealous, aren't you? Cause he loves me more.

MOTHER: Me jealous of you? How pathetic!
You're nothing, nothing at all.

SALLY: Yeah, and you keep telling me that so
that I never will be anything. *(Starts to cry.)* We've
got to get help . . . maybe therapy . . .

MOTHER: Therapy, my ass! What *we* need is for
you to shape up . . . or get out.

*(Sally goes to hit her mother, then turns away.
She sees the basement door is open, and walks
over.)*

SALLY: This should be locked. *(Tries to lock it.
A man suddenly pushes the door open and enters.
His clothes are torn and dirty; he looks like a dere-
lict. Sally hits him on the head.)*

SALLY: Mother, help!

MAN: No, wait, I just want . . .

MOTHER: You handle it, little Miss Know-It-All.

SALLY: Get out, get out! Mother, please, help
me!

*(Sally keeps hitting the man over the head, sob-
bing as she begs her mother for help. Her mother
just watches and laughs. The man tries to talk but
his words are drowned out by her screams. He
tries to shield himself from her blows, but finally
falls down, unconscious.)*

SALLY: Oh God, we've got to call the cops. I
need a phone booth, and some change.

MOTHER: Oh no, I'm not giving you any money.

SALLY: What's wrong with you? This guy could
kill you and you're laughing!

MOTHER: He doesn't want me, Sally, he wants
you.

*(Sally runs to a phone booth; a woman is using
the phone.)*

SALLY: Please, I need the phone . . .

WOMAN: Can't you see, I'm using it!

SALLY: Please, it's an emergency!

WOMAN: We all have problems. Now go away!

SALLY: But you don't understand. . . .

WOMAN: I don't want to understand! Now, leave me alone!

(Sally finds another phone. She desperately searches through her pockets for money; her fingers tremble and she's crying.)

SALLY: Oh, do I have a quarter? Where is it? *(She finds a quarter but her hands are shaking so much that she drops it.)* Damn! *(She picks it up. Her trembling hands make it hard for her to put it in the slot.)* Come on, come on . . . *(She gets it in and waits a second. The phone doesn't work and she hits it.)* Jesus Christ, I don't believe it! The phone doesn't work! *(She hits it again.)*

TELEPHONE: Ow! Don't hit me! That won't make me work.

SALLY: *(shaking it)* What's wrong with you? Why don't you work?

TELEPHONE: Maybe there's nothing wrong with me. Maybe it's you. Calm down and try again. And don't hit me.

SALLY: *(She is crying hard as she puts in the quarter again.)* Come on! Information, somebody, answer me! Help me!

TELEPHONE: I'm trying, I'm trying.

SALLY: Operator! Where's the operator, God damn it! Why can't you answer the phone? Why isn't it working? Why isn't anything working?

At the end of the exercise, the group members sat down to share their experiences of the dream. The dreamer, Sally, was quite shaken; she had really let herself go during this exercise, and her panic and pain were very real. The woman who played her mother instinctively put her arms around her, and the whole group acted to soothe and comfort her. The following is each group member's expression of what his or her dream character was feeling.

SALLY: I felt alone, totally helpless and power-less, like everything in the world was against me. And I felt that there must be something very deep, very fundamentally wrong with me for this to be so, because it seemed like I was the only one that the world wanted to destroy. And it was strange because even though I was so angry at my mother, all I could think about was trying to protect her. I was more afraid for her than I was for myself. But I felt I couldn't do anything for either of us. Everything I did was wrong or didn't work.

MOTHER: I was feeling jealous of my daughter. The whole thing with the sweaters was that my daughter looked better in them than I did, because she was younger and had a prettier body. I felt that I was having a bad relationship with my husband and couldn't do anything to make it better, so I took it out on my daughter, who I felt had the good relationship with my husband that was being de-nied me. I felt revenge when the derelict came in and I didn't do anything, as if maybe if she were destroyed, the love my husband felt for her would be given to me. But I was also horrified at myself, because my pride wouldn't let me put my arms around her and say, "I'll help you."

MAN: I was very angry and resentful. I wasn't a derelict; I had just been mugged and I wanted help. And you just beat me up. You didn't listen to me or even see me as a person; I was just this horrible object you had to destroy. You were never in any danger, but you were the center of attention. I was in danger, and I got hurt even worse and then was ignored.

WOMAN: I was angry that this woman would automatically assume that her problems were more important than mine. I didn't know what was wrong with her, but she didn't know what my problem was either, why *I* was on the phone. I felt a little sad at having to turn her away, and was mad that she put me in a position of having to do it so harshly and repeatedly, so that I ended up feeling guilty. And yet I knew that what I was doing on the phone was very important, too.

TELEPHONE: I felt frustrated that I didn't work. But I wasn't sure if it was me, or if she just wasn't operating me right. I didn't feel broken and I wanted to help her; I really wanted to know whether it was my fault or hers. I felt guilty for not doing my job, and helpless.

This exercise, and the responses of the group members, provided Sally with some major revelations about the way she handled the problems in her life. While there was no denying that certain real problems existed (as exemplified by her relationship with her mother), she saw that some of the choices she made in terms of dealing with those problems only exacerbated them. Through understanding the Man's true identity, she became aware of how her panic caused her to misinterpret situations and to perceive problems as worse than they were, setting her off in unnecessary and painful directions. The experience with the Woman at the telephone booth showed her how she compounded the frustrations in her life by hanging on and trying to force solutions from unlikely sources instead of accepting a given dead end and moving on to situations that offer the possibility of fulfillment. She also realized that she might not be using the tools accessible to her in the most productive ways. This dream exercise, though initially painful, provided her with specific insights as to how she could more effectively deal with the inevitable, and often unresolvable, problems of life.

Not long after doing this dream exercise, Sally was able to use these insights actively in her waking life. She received a bank notice saying that a large check she had deposited had bounced, and she immediately panicked because she had written a number of checks against that money. She rushed to her bank, collared a bank officer, and began frantically insisting that the bank delay paying off her checks or cover them until she got another check to deposit. The bank officer explained that this was impossible, and she became hysterical and hostile, berating him until he was on the verge of just walking away from her.

In the middle of her tirade she saw that she was getting nowhere, and recognized her behavior pattern from her dream. To the surprise of the bank officer, she abruptly stopped talking. She took a few seconds to compose herself, apologized to him, then started the conversation again in a much calmer tone. She explained the situation to him, and, instead of demanding that he do what she wanted, asked him what he thought she should do. The bank officer was mollified by her change in attitude and was much more inclined to help her. He asked her some questions, got all the facts he needed, then called the other bank to see why the check had bounced. He learned that at the time the check had been put through, the funds from an out-of-state check deposited into the account had not yet been collected. The money was there now, however, and the bank officer told Sally that the check could safely be redeposited and that none of the checks she had written would bounce.

Sally totally credits the dream exercise for enabling her to change her response to a problematic situation so that she could produce a positive outcome.

You can give added dimension to the experience of acting out your dream by first recreating as much as possible the circumstances and emotions that occurred the night you had the dream. This can take the form of your visualizing the room in which you had the dream, talking about the events of that day, reenacting conversations you had prior to going to bed, remembering your thoughts before falling asleep, etc. It doesn't matter whether you had the dream last night or five years ago. The closer you can come to feeling the way you did the night you had the dream, the more you will receive from subsequently acting it out.

10

Draw Your Dream Images

*T*here are occasions when pictures are a
more direct route than words for expressing the key
message of a dream. Freud recognized this when he
wrote, "Part of the difficulty of giving an account of
dreams is due to our having to translate these images
into words. 'I could draw it,' a dreamer often says to us,
'but I don't know how to say it.'"¹ Jung elaborated that
idea by declaring painting to be a more direct means than
words for dealing with unconscious non-verbal experi-
ence.² He often encouraged his patients to express their
fantasies and dreams in pictures. Both Freud and Jung
realized that dreams were pictures of feelings and sensations. In "Diary of Discovery: The Dream Journal," I
encouraged you to draw your symbols in your symbol
dictionary whenever possible. The reason for this is simple: drawing is a direct route to the unconscious, and

thus can reveal aspects of an image that words alone cannot. In addition, the drawing can elicit new and unexpected associations.

For my doctoral dissertation, I conducted a study in 1981 to determine the effect drawing has in psychoanalytic treatment, and discovered that drawing could express messages not yet evident to the conscious mind. I found numerous examples among my patients where drawing preceded and stimulated the conscious recognition of sensations, feelings, and thoughts.[3]

E X E R C I S E 1 8

Turn Your Dream into Pictures

Drawing, like dreaming, is a function of the right brain; it stimulates the brain to perform intuitively and simultaneously. Speech is a function of the left brain, motivating it to operate logically and linearly. Therefore, the combination and interaction of drawing and speech creates a fuller, richer experience since it utilizes both hemispheres of the brain. Through drawing your dream images you can make contact with parts of yourself that may be incomprehensible now, and then later, through written and verbal exercises with these images, come to understand these puzzling parts of yourself.

Here's a good example of what can happen when a dreamer draws important symbols from his dream. The dreamer, a victim of AIDS (Acquired Immune Deficiency Syndrome) and Kaposi's sarcoma (a form of cancer), had the following dream during a difficult bout with his illness:

Life and Death

A handsome dark-haired man, dressed in a white
T-shirt, white chinos, and black boots, is sitting on
a motorcycle. The motorcycle has a sidecar and in
the seat of it is a shriveled-up, ancient nun in her
black and gray habit. She's about one-third his size
and is sitting with her hands crossed; she is trian-
gularly shaped. He is magnificent. She is sickly,
withered, weathered, and barely alive.

It's night. Following them is a dark Darth
Vader-type character [the half-human, half-robot
villain of the *Star Wars* trilogy] on a black motorcycle, to which the man in white seems to be attached.

This monster is all in black; it's as if he's made
out of leather and metal. He has sharp white teeth
in a retractable jaw which can extend an arm's
length. His eye slits reveal flickering black light
and he wears a helmet. His hands are encased in
gloves and he wears black boots.

Between the two motorcycles, I see myself with
nine spirits. They seem to be large and slender and
have many different powers. I don't even know
about some of the powers, and yet I have control
over them. The spirits are offering diversionary
and protective tactics to the man in white, but the
monster is in hot pursuit and won't be diverted.

The chase seems to be on a dark country road,
maybe a secondary highway, but suddenly we
come to the city. As the man in white pulls to a
stop at a subway station, the monster is fairly close
behind. The subway station is a typical New York
one with dark green-black metal railings and fenc-
ing around it.

The monster gets off his motorcycle, threatening to attack. I'm not sure who the monster is going

to attack. I try to prevent him from doing so. I have the distinct feeling that I want the man in white to take the nun into the subway and let the spirits and me deal with the monster. But when he attacks the monster, I order the spirits to take the nun into the subway, where I assume there are other people.

The dreamer reported that he awoke from this dream very slowly. He wanted to reenter it but was able only to return to a state where he could see vibrations without seeing an image.

As he told me the dream, I became aware that there were two images in the dream that represented illness and death; I asked him to draw the nun (Figure 2) and the monster (Figure 3). What happened in the process

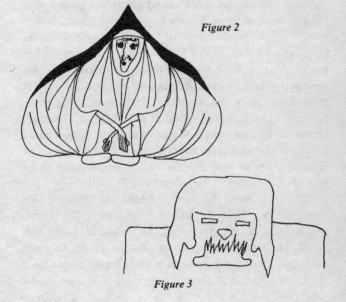

Figure 2

Figure 3

underscores the unique ability drawing a dream symbol has for advancing the dreamer in his understanding of his dreams. The nun turned into an onion as he was drawing it, and this became the clue to unraveling the dream's meaning. This meaning became clearer as the dreamer, using the gestalt technique of becoming the dream element (in this case, the nun/onion), uttered the following words:

"I am withered, dry, and dying. I am being chased. I am wrinkled and furrowed, squashed and misshapen. I am gray and old, rotting and decayed. I am being carried by someone magnificent. I am being taken to some place and am afraid. I grow underground, dark and damp. I am smelly. Cut me open and my sting brings tears to your eyes. I come apart and spread my poison. I am cancer."

The dreamer then became the monster, and said:

"I am ancient and timeless and older than human. But I am in modern form. I chew and cripple. I hurt. Somehow I don't always seem to be evil. Maybe I am an amoral force that works for a darker force, or darker forces. I am stubborn and determined to complete my destructive task. I have weight and armor but I am not invincible. Oddly, in spite of my frightening appearance, the man in white is not afraid of me. Although I cannot terrorize, I can damage. My powers seem to be limited only to a physical level beyond which I can't operate or reason. I am so machine-like that I almost seem to be part of or attached to the motorcycle."

After becoming the two elements, the dreamer said thoughtfully, "Now I think I know what the dream means. I think it's describing AIDS and Kaposi's sarcoma. The nun/onion represents the cancer, the Kaposi's sarcoma. The man in white is a white blood corpuscle. I think he's carrying the cancer in his sidecar to the lymph system, as represented by the subway. And the monster on the motorcycle is the AIDS. I think this describes how AIDS works. AIDS attacks the immune system while the lymph system is doing its job. The white corpuscle and the spirits are part of the immune system. But the white corpuscle didn't succeed in doing its job of getting rid of the cancer properly because it was distracted by the AIDS. The white corpuscle wasn't able to place it in the lymph system so that it could be disposed of."

Before he drew the image, the nun had no meaning for him except as something old and dying. It was only when it became an onion in the experience of drawing it that the associations to underground, spreading, and poison revealed themselves—associations that were instantly understood by him to represent cancer.

This man's dream reflects his deep-rooted desire to win the battle to rid himself of his disease. Understanding his dream made him aware that his unconscious is clearly on his side, supporting his wish to survive. He now knows he has a powerful helper deep within himself. Recent research has proven that feelings of helplessness, and conversely a profound desire to survive, directly affect the body's ability to reject cancerous tumors.[4]

Many people have dreams that reveal processes going on in their bodies that they aren't consciously aware of yet; as I mentioned in Chapter 1, Russian doctors have done research on this. At the time of this dream, the dreamer had a bad cough, which was worrying his doctors; they feared pneumonia. For a person with AIDS, where the immune system isn't functioning properly, pneumonia is especially dangerous. The doctors wanted to hospitalize him, but he refused and gave himself a nutrition treatment instead. His dream encouraged him by symbolically telling him that his white corpuscles were working and attacking the virus. Soon, he began to feel better and his cough eventually disappeared altogether.

I later asked him to complete the dream, and this was his ending: "I would have the man in white take the nun into the subway and see her on the way while the spirits and I take care of the monster." Perhaps in this dream lies a clue to the baffling new illness which is threatening to become a national epidemic.

A second dreamer, a woman, was ambivalent about marrying her fiancé. She reported the following dream, of which she remembered only a fragment, and then used the drawing technique to help her clarify her feelings.

Kissed by a Unicorn

I am with my possible future employer, and he is showing me my office-to-be. Outside is a lush green hill that looks beautiful under a cloudless blue sky. There are two levels, like plateaus, near the top of the hill. A piano is on each level. I am sitting with this man, who is ostensibly showing an interest in me that is connected with the job. I am uncomfortable with him and feel ambivalent toward him. A unicorn comes to the fence next to us and the unicorn and I kiss on the lips. My lips are closed. It is a blissful feeling, which immediately disappears when the man comments that it was not a unicorn that kised me but a goat. I open my eyes, see he is right, and am deflated.

When I initially asked the woman what she thought her dream meant, she said she believed it depicted a chronic problem of hers, her tendency to undermine a positive experience (the unicorn) by calling it something inferior (the goat). I then asked her to draw the unicorn (Figure 4) and the goat (Figure 5). When she finished, the dream's true meaning manifested itself to her. The horn on the unicorn made her think of a penis; kissing the unicorn in the dream symbolizing sexual feelings toward a potent man. The man she was engaged to in real life, she realized, was the goat and had no penis in the sense that he was weak and unassertive, not what she desired in a man. The dream helped her resolve her am-

Figure 4

Figure 5

bivalence toward him. Although she was eager to get married, she decided it was wiser to stay single until the right man came along.

Another good example of drawing the dream image to clarify a key feeling occurred with this male patient's dream:

Applying the Brakes

I am in a large department store, maybe Bloomingdale's. I'm trying to go down the escalator; there's something very frightening about it. The floor below looks slippery; I'm afraid I won't be able to stop when I reach the floor and will uncontrollably slide across it, knocking things over and embarrassing myself. A topless, sexy blonde girl gives me her bicycle. She is friendly but is also friendly to others so I don't think there's anything personal about it. I'm afraid to go down the escalator on the bicycle so I go down on foot instead. I squeeze the rubber handrail so hard that it becomes as thin as spaghetti, and I can't hold on to it. Later I realize that I could have gone down on the bicycle if I had kept applying the brakes at intervals.

When I asked the patient his thoughts about the dream, he told me he had just started going out with a new woman whom he liked very much. Since they hadn't been seeing each other for more than a few weeks, he thought he might be scared of liking her too much in relation to how long he knew her, and might uncontrollably fall in love and get hurt. I then asked him to draw the escalator (Figure 6). What was immediately evident in the drawing is that the escalator didn't end at the floor, but rather dropped off sharply into an abyss;

Figure 6.

the patient described it as the way escalator stairs disappear as soon as they touch a surface. He suddenly realized that his real fear was that he wouldn't fall in love and complete his feeings for this woman but would instead cut off and distance himself from her. The fact that she was an ideal peson for him left him with no excuse to hide behind if the relationship didn't work out; he would have to confront his fear of intimacy.

Not every dream lends itself to this exercise. The dream must have one or more vivid symbols or images for the exercise to work. But when it does work, it often works immediately and dramatically because the pictured image can unveil something that the mental image does not convey. For example, the first dreamer *thought* of the image of the nun; it became an onion only when he drew it, leading him to the association of cancer. The second dreamer, before drawing, thought her dream was merely corroborating a trait in herself of which she was already aware; only when she drew the images did she realize that the meaning of the dream lay in the pictured difference between the unicorn and the goat. For the third dreamer, drawing the image provided an opposite, and more accurate, interpretation than his initial one.

So use this exercise when your dreaming mind offers you intriguing images. Don't censor yourself as you draw. If you start to draw an image and it becomes something else (like the nun turning into an onion), follow through on that new image. Like the dreamer in the first example, you might also find it stimulating to use the gestalt exercise of becoming the element with your picture. And don't get caught up in the "I can't draw" syndrome. This isn't a test of artistic merit but rather a new way for you to experience a dream image.

Creativity, Lucidity, and Nightmares

The Creativity That Lies Hidden in Your Dreams

The dreamwork-creativity connection

Dreams are our most intimate creations. A universal phenomena, they are testimony to the creative potential within us all. Like a work of art, they contain a unique language of imagery and metaphor expressed within a specific structure. These symbols aren't chosen from our conscious minds, as they are in artistic endeavors, but we *do* create them; they are the products of our unconscious.

Since the publication of Freud's *The Interpretation of Dreams* in 1900, there has been a growing awareness that the imagery and the mechanisms at work in our unconscious dreaming are identical to the ones we consciously draw upon in a creative act.

G. K. Chesterton wrote, "The original quality in any man of imagination is imagery. It is a thing like the landscape of his dreams. . . . This general atmosphere, and pattern or structure of growth, governs all his creations, however varied."[1] Creativity and dreaming are inextricably intertwined; they are both functions of the right brain, using the same well of memory, wisdom, and personal symbolism, and they both spring from the unconscious. In dreams, the raw feelings are thrown up in a haphazard, symbolic form. In a creative endeavor, the same material is consciously transformed, through the disciplines of the particular medium and the creator's individual sensibilities, into a work of art.

Ultimately, the creativity involved in both dreamwork and works of art entails the same process: self-discovery. Self-discovery can do a lot more than just inform us; it has the ability to transform us as well. Any search within ourselves will inevitably reveal anger, guilt, insecurity, and so forth—feelings that when not expressed consume tremendous energy and keep us stuck in unproductive patterns of behavior. The creative process, expressed through either artistic or dreamwork activities, gives us the opportunity to acknowledge these feelings and convert them into something positive, thus freeing both the feelings and the energy entrapped in them. Once this energy is released, it can then be used for positive, creative tasks. The Senoi recognized this and channelled the energy freed in their conquering-the-enemy technique into creative products. In this way, helplessness can be transformed into power, and there's the added bonus of the exhilaration that comes from making something concrete from inner intangibles. Dreams, through their direct channel to the unconscious, can be a powerful catalyst for creativity. The dreamwork exercises in this chapter can help you to get the full benefit of this valuable inner resource.

I've had many reports from students and patients of

the ways their involvement in dreamwork has heightened their creativity in general. A writer remarked that ever since she started working with her dreams her productivity, in terms of the number of new story ideas conceived during a given period of time, dramatically increased in a way she'd never experienced before. Not only was the quantity of ideas enhanced, but also the variety of their themes, the richness and originality of their details, and the ease in which they developed into full stories. An artist also commented that his dreamwork has measurably increased his creative output. Where once he suffered through recurring dry spells of creative blocks, he now enjoys a plethora of artistic ideas, often based on an image, shape, color, or mood from one of his dreams. He finds it enormously useful to paste photographs and other visual images into his dream journal; their relationship to his dream often inspires him in a whole new direction.

It's important not to limit the concept of creativity to just those disciplines considered to be "the arts": literature, theater, dance, music, visual art, etc. Creativity extends to the way we live our lives, make decisions, and handle our relationships and careers. Creativity entails extracting from ourselves that which is unique to us, different from the familiar and commonplace, in a form or manner that satisfies our individual needs. What better task to use this insight and information than the primary one we all share: traveling the journey that is our life? In this chapter, I will introduce exercises that will enable you to use your dreams to get creative solutions to problems in your work and life.

Solving problems without
even trying

The unconscious mind, through dreams, often provides the answer to a problem even without prompting. This can occur when the dreamer is consciously and intensely immersed in a task or problem that demands a creative solution. In his book *The Courage to Create*, the psychoanalyst Rollo May writes that it's no accident that answers to problems come when the mind is at rest, especially in areas in which the person has worked "laboriously and with dedication." Our neurological thought processes continue even when we are not aware of them.[2]

Elias Howe's unconscious, through a nightmare, enabled him to finally complete his invention of the sewing machine. He had worked for years on it, but couldn't figure out where to put the eye in the sewing-machine needle. He had a nightmare in which savages captured him and, with spears raised, ordered him to complete the invention or they would kill him. Staring in terror at the sharp heads of the spears, he noticed eye-shaped holes near the tips. He then realized that there was the solution to his problem; he could put the eye near the point of the needle. Upon awakening he implemented the idea, and provided the world with a tool of inestimable value.

Another example occurred in the work of the German chemist Friedrich Kekule von Stradonitz. He struggled for many years to find the molecular structure of benzene. One evening, while working on the unresolved problem, he dozed off and had a dream about atoms forming long chains and twisting and turning like snakes. One of the snakes took hold of its own tail, and Kekule awoke with excitement. He realized from his dream that the structure of benzene was a closed carbon ring. This discovery revolutionized modern chemistry.

Dr. Niels Bohr developed the theory that electrons revolve around atoms from a dream in which planets attached by strings were circling around the sun.

In 1903, Otto Loewi speculated that nervous impulses were transmitted chemically rather than electrically, but could not find a way to prove it. Seventeen years later, he had a dream in which an experimental design appeared that could test his theory. When he awakened he performed the experiment. It was a success, and he was finally able to prove his hypothesis, eventually winning a Nobel Prize for his work.

Bertrand Russell would often work hard on an abstract mathematical or physical problem to the point of exhaustion, and then go to sleep. He frequently got the answer to his problem in his dream. Albert Einstein's theory of relativity came to him while he was dozing, and René Descartes's rationalistic theory appeared in a dream.

From the above illustrations, it's clear that dreams express their messages in symbolic language and a myriad of forms. If the dreamer is in tune with his own unconsciousness, he may be able to decipher the not-so-obvious meaning; dreamwork can aid everyone in interpreting these messages. However, some creative products have come from dreams that were translated directly into music, words, pictures, or whatever the dreamer's medium was. For example, the eighteenth-century Italian violinist and composer Guiseppe Tartini dreamed that he handed his violin to the Devil; the Devil then proceeded to play a sonata of great beauty. When he awoke, Tartini wrote down the sonata as he remembered it in his dream, calling it the "Devil's Sonata." Though he believed it was the best sonata he had ever written, he said it didn't match the one he heard in his dream.

Steve Allen wrote a song in one of his dreams in 1954. He remembered, upon awakening, what was to become his greatest hit: "This Could Be the Start of Something Big." Richard Wagner's opera *Tristan und Isolde* was the product of a dream. He also had composed the prelude to *Das Rheingold* during a state of drowsiness.

Robert Louis Stevenson suffered from nightmares in both his childhood and adult life. To put himself to sleep, he concocted tales to entertain himself; when he decided to use this talent professionally, his nightmares ceased. His dreams then began to supply him with marketable stories, and he claimed these tales were often better than the ones he created in his waking state. His classic novel, *Dr. Jekyll and Mr. Hyde*, came from a dream that he elaborated on with his conscious mind.

Samuel Taylor Coleridge's lavish *Kubla Khan* was written from images that came to him in a dream state. It's said that the housekeeper walked into the room while he was transferring the dream to paper to ask him if he wanted tea, and the whole last verse vanished forever. The earliest Greek dramas drew their plots from the structure of dreams, and Feodor Dostoyevsky and James Joyce also wrote from their dreams, and Voltaire composed poetry while dreaming.

Not only artists and inventors can find answers in their dreams. Jack Nicklaus improved his golf game, which had been in a slump, by using a new grip that appeared to him in a dream.

A problem doesn't have to be of monumental importance to be solved in a dream. A woman told me about an evening she spent searching through cookbooks and her recipe files to find a special dish for her sister-in-law's Labor Day party. She found nothing that excited her, and finally went to bed. She dreamed that night of being in an elegant ballroom with long tables against the walls. On the tables were huge crystal bowls filled with a beautiful salad. She looked at it closely, and saw that it was made of elbow macaroni, sliced tomato, sliced raw zucchini, red onion, and parsley. The macaroni was a pale pink, and she was struck by how pretty all the colors looked together. She tasted it and noticed it had a vinegary tang. When she awoke from the dream she scribbled it down and the next day recreated it, using a red wine vinegar dressing to turn the macaroni pink. It looked and tasted just the way it had in her dream, so she dubbed it her "Dream Pasta Salad."

Make your dream work for you

E X E R C I S E   1 9

Incubation

There's no need to wait passively for your dreams to resolve your problems; you can learn to direct them to come forth with solutions. The exercise is an expanded version of the incubation method mentioned in the "Dream Journal" chapter.

While lying in bed at night, consciously work on or think about the particular problem you want to solve; it can be in any area from work to relationships—personal, creative, and otherwise. What do you want to achieve? What obstacles stand in your way? What solutions have you tried? What would happen if you did achieve your goal? What assumptions about the problem have you made that might limit your choice of solutions? After thoroughly examining the problem, formulate a single clear, concise question. The exercise hinges on asking the right question; if initially you don't get an answer, try rewording the question.

As you start to fall asleep and enter the hypnogogic state, repeat the question to yourself and tell yourself that you want to get the answer in your dreams. Then write down any dreams you have, even if they don't seem pertinent. Upon closer examination you may find they contain information that could change your entire perception of the problem itself.

It's very important to want truly the answer you're requesting. As a writer learned, you cannot fool the unconscious. She had been trying to develop a commercial story idea for a television movie—a form of writing for which she felt great ambivalence. Unable to come up with anything both salable and interesting, she decided to try this technique. She diligently worked on it before going to bed, itemizing all the characteristics of a successful television movie, then went to sleep telling herself she would answer in her dreams the question, "What is the ideal story for a television movie?". That night, she dreamed that her apartment was filled with filthy, overflowing cat litter boxes. She laughed as she wrote down the dream the next morning; her unconscious mind clearly reflected her opinion of television movies and thus refused to work on them.

She successfully used the exercise, however, on a piece she did care about. She was working on an action-adventure movie and needed to flesh out the personality of her lead woman character, an agent for a secret international antiterrorist organization on an important mission. Again, she worked on it before going to bed and fell asleep asking herself, "What is this character's background?" She had an elaborate, exciting dream about her parents being glamorous international spies. She awoke with the instant knowledge that she had just what she needed. She could strengthen the woman's commitment to her mission by making her parents two of the famous World War II spies who founded the organization after the war to preserve world peace.

This exercise is equally effective with "life" problems. An older woman used it in dealing with a major personal crisis. She had recently put herself through college by doing secretarial work, and had graduated with a degree in finance. She then went to work for a savings and loan bank, where she had a malicious supervisor who seemed dedicated to making her life miserable. The woman was in a terrible quandary; she couldn't bear to remain at her job, and yet felt she was too old to get another one somewhere else. She saw no way out of the situation and, having just learned the incubation exercise, decided to see if her dreams could offer her any alternatives. She went to sleep one night asking herself, "What should I do about my job?" and had the following dream:

What Should I Do About My Job?

I am on a chair in a cage in a laboratory filled with experimental animals. I am in the largest cage. The attendant, dressed in a white coat, is my boss at the bank. He is feeding the animals, but does not bring me any food. I am trapped and starving.

There is a door in the room and I hear the sounds of cutlery and female voices, as if there's a restaurant right outside. I wonder what's going on. Suddenly the wall disappears, and I'm looking into what appears to be a company cafeteria. I recognize the women eating there; I knew them when I worked as a secretary to put myself through college. I wake up.

She awoke from the dream with the realization that even if she couldn't immediately get another job in this field, she could still support herself as a secretary. Her anxiety left her when she saw that she was not trapped between being miserable and starving; her dream had pointed out another option. She called a stockbroker friend and told him she had made the decision to quit her job and go back to office work until she found an opening in a good brokerage firm. He told her he had heard of an opening at a small but prestigious company. She applied, and a week later had the exact job she had always wanted. She credits the dream with giving her the alternative that empowered her to quit; it was that decision that led to her new job.

E X E R C I S E   2 0

Self-Hypnosis

You can get the feeling of a dream state even while awake. A simple relaxation exercise can enable you to establish that kind of connection between your conscious and unconscious minds whenever you so desire. Images and ideas that arise during this experience can be used to create your paintings, poetry, songs, dances, inventions, etc. When tried in conjunction with the incubation method, this exercise is excellent in solving problems. Quite a few of my students have commented that this is one of the most potent, productive techniques they've used.

The best way to do this exercise is first to tape-record it, and then play it back when you want to have the experience. Since its purpose is to relax you, it should be recorded in a slow, soothing voice, with plenty of pauses. It's also helpful to play tranquil, meditative music in the background. Start with just the music playing for a minute, then record the following:

Self-Hypnosis Exercise

Close your eyes and sit with your legs uncrossed and your feet flat on the floor. Prepare yourself to take five deep breaths. You will inhale as deeply as you can, hold the breath for a count of five, then exhale as completely as you can.... Inhale.... One, two, three, four, five, exhale.... Inhale.... One, two, three, four, five, exhale. ...Inhale.... One, two, three, four, five, exhale.... Inhale.... One, two, three, four, five, exhale.... Inhale.... One, two, three, four, five, exhale....

Feel your body get heavier and heavier.... Feel yourself sinking deeper and deeper into the chair.... Let your mind relax and go.... Know that your mind contains all the imagery and answers you will ever need....

Now feel yourself floating, on an air mattress in a calm sea.... Floating and drifting, floating and drifting, floating and drifting.... Let go of the conscious control of your mind and allow your unconscious to take over.... Know there is great freedom when your intuition takes charge; spontaneous and innovative ideas appear.... Let them come forth.... Then let them go....

As you float, your body becomes more and more relaxed.... Your muscles become slack and heavy, slack...and heavy.... Your breathing slows down.... Your heart rate slows down.... Your body winds down and down.... Starting with your head, feel your scalp and forehead relax and expand.... The warm relaxation spreads down your cheeks...into your jaw; let your mouth drop open.... The warm, heavy feeling extends to your shoulders, pulling them down...and into your arms...and your hands...and all of your fingers.... All feeling relaxed, and warm, and easy...

The easy warmth spreads down through your chest...relaxing your diaphragm.... Breathe slowly, evenly, easily.... Feel your back relax, expand.... Sink down into the floating air mattress.... Feel the relaxation move down into your thighs...your knees...your calves...your toes.... All relaxing, expanding, warm...

As you float, your mind drifts.... Everything around you disappears, even the sound of this tape.... Your free, spontaneous mind takes over and everything else disappears....

Let your mind go...float...drift...

When you finish recording the words, continue recording the music. While listening to your tape, your mind can freely wander, creating symbols and images and solving problems.

After you do the exercise, write down the images, thoughts, memories, insights, stories, etc., that occurred during the exercise. The symbols that appear are part of your own personal language and contain not-yet-conscious meanings that can aid you in your quest for self-discovery. You may also want to use these images in a creative task.

One dreamer was given the premise for a play by doing this exercise. Without any preconceived ideas about what he wanted to experience, he put himself into this hypnotic state and had the following "dream" experience.

Last of the Hobos

It's an early, gray morning at a Midwestern railroad yard. Cargo is loaded and unloaded. An old hobo warms himself in front of a trashcan fire; his face is smudged with soot.

Suddenly I (but younger, like a novice journalist) am talking to him; we both eat soup out of the can. It's grown dark; the trashcan fire provides the main light. The hobo talks about his life and how things have changed; fewer men ride the rails these days and they're a much different breed. He says a hobo's life is a barometer for what's happening in the rest of the world. He talks of the people he's known and things he's seen, and his tales have a mythic quality. There's something wise and almost mystical about him, and I'm fascinated. I make him my mentor, and consider traveling with him. He says that sometimes a person has to be impulsive and act on the moment. It's like jumping a freight train. If you hesitate just a second before grabbing onto the rail, you'll miss the train or get pulled under. I decide to go on one journey with him, and we jump on a train together.

When the dreamer emerged from this relaxed state, he realized he had created an interesting dramatic situation. He was intrigued by the contrast between the old, worldly wise man and the young, impressionable one and was curious as to where their relationship might lead. He had always been fascinated by the hobo life-style, immersing himself in Woody Guthrie lore when he was a teenager. He subsequently wrote a play about the journey the old man and young journalist take together.

Other dreamers have reported during this exercise strong visual images which they later painted and drew. A clothing designer said he saw a whole collection of dresses, as if he had been seated at a fashion show. The dresses had unusual, angular lines, and he incorporated some of these features into his waking-life designs.

Whether it's through art or dreamwork, expressing these images from your unconscious can transform and empower you, bringing you closer to the full utilization of your potential.

12

Awake in a Dream: Lucid Dreaming

M ost of us have very little control over the majority of our dreams; our unconscious takes us on a journey, and it's not until we awaken that we realize that we never left our beds. Lucid dreams are a notable exception to this rule, for in lucid dreams we know that we are dreaming while we are in the dream. This awareness opens up a myriad of possibilities; we can influence the dream's direction, control and change the dream ego, and call back dream characters.

There are different levels of lucid dreaming. The most intense lucid dreams have been compared to psychedelic experiences and mystic states. The dreamer may find himself bathed in white light or see brilliant colors. Objects and situations may take on a heightened reality and the clarity of detail can be extraordinarily vivid. There may be an expanded sense of time and space, accompanied by feelings of deep pleasure. Some lucid dreams have been referred to as altered states of consciousness. The dreamer may leave his body and travel to different places and times, into the past or the future, as well as be able to move through solid objects such as walls and glass. This is the same experience believers in the occult refer to as out-of-body travel or astral projection.[1]

Even lucid dreams that aren't quite that intense still differ significantly from ordinary dreams. With the exception of common lucid dream maneuvers such as flying and moving through time and space, lucid dreams tend to be more realistic than ordinary ones; dream characters usually behave in their customary, waking life fashion. It's been proven that time is the same in lucid dreams as it is in waking life; counting to five requires the same duration of time in both states of consciousness.[2] Sensations, such as taste, odor, and touch, are heightened and memory and analytic thought are sharper than in ordinary dreams. Specific details of lucid dreams, however, can still be unrealistic.

In the last five or six years, much research has been done on lucid dreams. A number of scientists have written their doctoral dissertations on them, and the subject has been popularized in magazines and on television and radio shows. Why all this interest? One reason is that a number of independent studies have shown a connection between mental health and lucid dreaming. A group of researchers has learned through their clinical studies that as people become more aware of their feelings, their dreams become more lucid.[3] The experimental psychologist Jayne Gackenbach has observed that lucid dreamers are usually less depressed and neurotic and have better self-esteem than nonlucid dreamers. She has found that while lucid dreamers don't usually partake in self-aware-ness exercises such as yoga and meditation, they still have a mystical awareness. "These are people...who seem to be at peace with their culture and its philoso-phies and religions."[4] Through further studies, Gacken-bach learned that lucid dreaming requires a good sense of emotional balance; the dreamer must be able to main-tain the degree of awareness necessary to know that he is dreaming without going too far and waking himself up. Lucid dreamers must also have a good physical sense of balance in order to fly. Her study of people walking on a balance beam showed that the more facile dreamers were better on it than the others.[5]

An English scientist, Keith Herne, has even invented a machine that he claims will enable people to have lucid dreams. The machine detects when the dreamer is enter-ing an REM state through the onset of rapid, irregular breathing, and then stimulates him with electric shocks. The jolts are at a level of intensity that, without waking him up, alerts the dreamer to the fact that he is dream-ing. At last hearing, the machine was being manufac-tured and would be made available to the public for under $100.[6]

Many people who have lucid dreams without being aware of their full potential use their ability to repeat or prolong pleasurable parts of the dream, especially sex-ual. This ability to stop a dream, alter it, repeat segments of it over and over, etc., until a "perfect" resolution is reached or total satisfaction achieved gives an indication of all that we can do with our lucid dreams if we so choose; the possibilities are limited only by the situa-tions presented by the unconscious.

One area in which lucid dreams can be especially

beneficial is in eliminating nightmares. Lucid dreams give us an opportunity to explore neglected parts of ourselves and to learn to deal with our fears; perhaps this is one reason lucid dreamers are said to be less neurotic than other people. If we're aware that we're dreaming, we know that no harm will come to us in situations of danger; however, this awareness does not mean that we don't feel afraid. What it gives us is an invaluable chance to learn to cope with our fear, to experience it fully instead of running away from it, so that we can handle it better in our waking lives. The Senoi aborigines stressed the importance of learning to fight one's enemies to the death in one's dreams. The benefits of experiencing fear this way are similar to those gained in therapy. The individual, through challenging and struggling with his fears, changes from being their victim to feeling his own power and strength; eventually he learns to diffuse his fears or make peace with them.

Yogi dreaming

Tibetan Buddhist monks, known as Yogis, are taught an extraordinary degree of dream control as part of their religious training. The Yogi's purpose is to free himself from the endless cycle of deaths and rebirths, so that he can achieve enlightenment, or "nirvana." He spends many highly disciplined years working with his guru to master the six doctrines that lead to ultimate knowledge. One of these doctrines is to control the dream state.

His object is to maintain an unbroken consciousness throughout both the waking and dreaming state. By controlling his dreams, the monk has the power to change dream forms. For example, he may change fire into water, or he may trample upon the fire because he knows he is dreaming. He can transform one object into several, or turn a small object into a large one.[7] The Yogi who has gained mastery over his waking and dreaming life has remarkable power indeed. His awareness that he need not fear his dream images because they are products of his own thoughts puts him in agreement with Freud, Jung, and Perls, all of whom concur that we are both creator of and actor in our dreams.

Using lucid dreams

Lucid dreams are not just useful with nightmares. They are helpful in learning new skills, getting over phobias, and solving problems. For example, a painter had developed a block that was preventing her from completing a picture. In a lucid dream, she found herself trying to walk to her easel, but her legs were paralyzed. She managed to force herself to the easel. The day after the dream, she was able to stand at her easel and complete her painting. It's important to see that actions carried out consciously in a dream can then be repeated in waking life.

Lucid dreams can also be used for creative purposes. Artists can memorize a beautiful scene presented in a dream and paint it later. A musician reports that he's able to compose melodies while lucid-dreaming, and then write them out when he awakes. A comedy writer uses the ability to repeat dream scenes to work on dialogue and jokes. He's able to switch set-up lines among the characters, have them try out different attitudes, and replay a scene over and over until a character says the right line. He says lucid dreaming is not only perfect for improvising, but that it's also an effortless way to polish a scene. The only drawback is that he has to stop himself from laughing out loud at the jokes because that wakes him up.

Learning to lucid-dream

At present, only about ten percent of the population can lucid-dream at will.[8] However, there are a number of ways that you can teach yourself to lucid-dream.

E X E R C I S E   2 1
Stephen LaBerge's MILD Technique

One exercise, by the lucid dream researcher Stephen La-Berge, is called Mnemonic Induction of Lucid Dreams (MILD). When you feel yourself awakening, try to focus your thoughts on the last dream you were having. Recall whatever details, feelings, experiences, etc., that you can. Then spend ten to fifteen minutes reading, meditating, or doing anything else that requires full wakefulness. What you do can also be related to what you want to dream. Then, while lying in bed, say to yourself, "The next time I dream, I want to recognize that I'm dreaming." Visualize your body lying in bed, sleeping. See yourself back in your last dream, or another dream; but *know* that you are dreaming. Repeat the affirmation and visualization until you feel your intention is firm, then let yourself fall back to sleep.[9]

The daughter of a Holocaust survivor used this exercise to turn the following recurring nightmare into a lucid dream.

The Nazis

I'm in Paris during World War II. A friend and I are taken to a small apartment by a young woman; it's one of the hideouts of the French Underground. She leaves us there. The apartment is clean and bare. Everything in the apartment—the beds, chests, tables, etc.—is bright red, blue, and yellow, the primary colors, and shaped like cubes and rectangles. It looks like a cubist painting. There are clothes for us to change into, and the walls are lined with bunk beds. We change clothes and go outside.

We wander around the streets of Paris. We hear air raid sirens; the Nazis are coming. There's mass panic in the streets as everyone runs for cover. We are lost. No one will let us into their house, and doors are shut in our faces. Soon we're the only ones left on the street. We should never have left the apartment because now we can't find our way back. I wake up.

When the dreamer awoke, she concentrated on remembering the details of the nightmare. She then spent fifteen minutes thinking about the dream and her mother's experience in a concentration camp. Next, she repeated over and over to herself that the next time she had a dream she wanted to know that she was dreaming. She visualized herself sleeping and back in the dream, aware that it was a dream. She reported that when she fell asleep again she reentered the dream and it became a lucid dream.

The Nazis (Lucid Dream)

I'm back on the empty streets in Paris; I see Nazi
tanks in the distance, approaching. I immediately
will both myself and my friend back to the cubist
apartment. There's a young man sleeping in one of
the bunk beds. He wakes up when we enter but
he's not surprised to see us; many people come and
go through the apartment. We hear heavy boot-
steps coming up the stairs—Nazis. There's an
escape hatch, a secret tunnel, in the apartment.
The young man shows us where it is. He tells us to
go with him; my friend wants to join him. I'm terrified and start to leave with them, but then I remember that I'm dreaming. I realize that if I stay, I
can do what I've always wanted to do—kill a
Nazi. The man and my friend don't know that
they're in a dream, and I decide that it's better to
let them escape. I don't want to have to worry
about saving them. I don't want anything to dis-
tract from the pleasure I'm going to get from killing
some Nazis. The man and my friend leave, and
there's loud banging at the door. I'm scared; I
know I'm dreaming and I have to struggle to keep
myself from waking up. The door explodes open,
and two Nazis burst in.

This is my chance. I don't see their faces, just
their uniforms. I attack them with incredible force
and strength, like a bull. I claw and kick and punch
and bite. One of them grabs me and holds me so
that I can't fight. I start to panic. Then I remember
that this is my dream, and I can have anything I
want. This gives me renewed strength. I break
free. I grab one Nazi by the balls and twist and pull
them till he screams in pain. He doubles over and I
smash him in the face and then hit him under the

chin so that he flies up into the air and crashes down. The other Nazi is paralyzed; I want to destroy them one at a time, without distraction. I go to the Nazi lying on the floor and stomp on his stomach and groin until he is smashed to bits.

Then I turn on the other Nazi. Now that I'm ready for him he comes to life again. He grabs me by the neck and tries to strangle me. I pull back his fingers until they break. I sink my teeth into his neck and bite his jugular vein. I'm like an animal, a wild boar; I have a primal urge to kill. I bite out most of his neck, blood spurts everywhere, all over me, dribbling down my chin. I love the feel of it, a Goddamn Nazi's blood all over me. I think of my mother, and all her relatives who died, and I rip him apart with my teeth like a tiger, almost devouring him. It's a thrilling, animal experience, even more intense than an orgasm. I feel as if I have within me all the power and life force of the six million who died. Finally the Nazi's body is emptied of blood, deflated. The young man and my friend come out of their hiding place. They are astonished. I look up and say, "You are not forgotten."

I then bring myself to full consciousness and wake up. I feel as if a huge store of anger that has been bottled up inside me has finally been released, and I savor my feelings of victory and strength and accomplishment.

After this cathartic experience, the dreamer never had this dream again.

E X E R C I S E   2 2

Look for Your Hands

Carlos Castaneda, in his book *Journey to Ixtlan*, writes that he was told that conscious dreaming is the path to power and was given a lucid dreaming exercise by the spiritual man Don Juan. He suggests to Castaneda that as he is about to fall asleep, he should tell himself to regard his hands in the dream and know that he is dreaming. He should next look at some other object in his environment for a moment or two, then bring his eyes back to his hands. (Of course, it doesn't have to be hands, it can be anything.) The goal is to be able to keep the image in one's awareness until it is clear and unshifting. Once a person can achieve this, according to Don Juan, he has the ability to select, reject, and choose those items which lead to power. To quote Don Juan, "In *dreaming*, you have power; you can change things; you may find out countless concealed facts; you can control whatever you want."[10]

The musician I mentioned before has had great success with this exercise. He often plays the piano in his dreams, and the sight of his fingers moving on the keys triggers his awareness that he's dreaming. He's then able to compose dream melodies that he can remember when he wakes up.

A student taught herself to associate the sight of her hands in a dream with the awareness that she was dreaming, and used it to transform this potentially bad dream into a pleasurable one.

Turning the Tables

I am flying. I land at the beach and a disgusting, macho man approaches me and starts coming on to me. He wants me to bring him to orgasm. I catch sight of my hands trembling and realize I'm dreaming. I turn the tables on him and force him to satisfy *me* sexually, by doing things he doesn't want to do, until I have an orgasm. Then I fly away, triumphant.

EXERCISE 23

Push Your Dream into Lucidity

By sharpening your awareness of prelucid states in your dreams, you may be able to push an ordinary dream into a lucid one. A prelucid state is a point in your dream when you suspect you might be dreaming. There are a number of common dream occurrences that can put you in a prelucid state; by alerting yourself to them and developing a critical attitude while in your dreams, you can take advantage of their appearance to treat yourself to a lucid dream.

Fear: Intense fear is a powerful catalyst for realizing that you're dreaming. A dream can simply be too frightening to believe; one dreamer reported that her scary dreams often became lucid because she would say to herself during the dream: "This *has* to be a nightmare. I hope to God this is a nightmare." Recognizing it as such usually woke her up. Though the natural tendency is to awaken, it's better to use your lucidity to work through your fear and resolve the situation.

In the following dream, a woman's fear made her realize that she was dreaming, and she used her lucidity to rescue herself.

I Have Disappeared from Life

I wake up in the late afternoon and hear my parents talking about my not being home. I am angry at them, but out of decency—so that they won't continue worrying—I ask them if they are looking for me. They are apparently worried. I ask what time it is; they say it is four o'clock on Tuesday. I begin to cry and say I missed four appointments I had that day because they didn't wake me up.

I say, crying, "You don't care." And they deny that. I realize it is four-thirty and I still have time to make my five o'clock appointment and my six o'clock one following it.

I want to dress quickly, but I find myself running on sand. I come to a patch of tall grass and flowers and playfully run through it rather than avoid it. Then I see that it is the garden in front of a modern office in the Hamptons. I hope they didn't see me as I ran through the garden because I partially destroyed it.

I am now in a deep hole in the sand and suddenly I realize I am trapped and there is nowhere to go. The only entrance/exit is about five feet above me. There may be a grating over it. I see a small child crawling over the grating and I call, but the child doesn't say anything. I hear people but I become too frightened to shout. I lose my voice. I wonder if my voice will return when I am desperate enough. I think of it growing dark and being stuck in this hole. I think of being one of the people who disappear and no one ever knows what happened to them. I'm so terrified, I suddenly realize that I'm dreaming. I wish very hard to be out of the hole, and I magically see myself rise up as if I am in an elevator. I am brought to the surface, and I walk away from the hole.

Recognizing the impossible: Identifying a dream's details as impossible or incongruous often leads to an awareness that you're dreaming, so it's important to try to be alert to these occurrences in your dreams. A man was recorded to have dreamed of a frightening school teacher who was eight feet tall moving menacingly toward him. At that instant, he remembered that this teacher, whom he knew in high school, was only four feet, eleven inches tall. He realized that he must be dreaming, and his dream became lucid.

This dream became lucid when the dreamer realized how bizarre one of the dream characters was:

Rhinoceros

I'm with my parents and my brother. The toilet is overflowing on a rug that is in my current apartment. This rug is not supposed to get wet. I feel intolerant toward someone, perhaps my brother, who is acting abnormal. Then I feel affection for him.

I meet up with a small pink and orange rhinoceros. I'm friendly to it, and it flutters its eyelashes. It has little flags, like wings, on its sides that go around in circles. When I notice these, I think, "Rhinos don't have wings," and I realize I'm dreaming.

That dreamlike feeling: Noticing that you're experiencing strange, dreamlike sensations can also catapult you into a lucid dream. This feeling can come from the events of the dream or your own mental and physical responses.

A dreamer pushed this dream into lucidity by identifying her experiences and perceptions as dreamlike.

Where Did the Prince Go?

I must save a prince from several men who are out to destroy him; he's a friend of mine. I run through the halls of the palace, which may be a movie theater, past movie poster ads, into a room. I hide the prince in the closet. Then I wonder if he will be safe there, and I stuff him into a laundry hamper; he's now only like a bunch of clothing.

The villains enter and we talk awhile. I think they were told to suspect me of trying to help the prince. I'm glad that they notice nothing. I then wonder if the prince would have lived if I had kept him in the closet. The men, I think, didn't open it.

I then take the prince out of the hamper but I find that I only have clothes there. The heart of the shirt is still beating. I realize a person with bones could never have fit into the hamper. I go to look in the closet, where I had left him before. But no, I hadn't merely undressed the prince; I had moved all that there was of him to the hamper.

I'm very confused by his dissolving, and rationalize that if I had done nothing the men would have destroyed him anyway. And maybe he's around here someplace. I think that all of this is very strange and baffling and feels unreal, like a dream. Then I realize it is a dream!

Recurrent dreams: Recognizing a dream as one you've had before can turn it into a lucid dream. Recurrent dreams are often intense, important ones expressing unresolved conflicts. Completing and resolving the dream will make it disappear.

A dreamer had had this dream on and off for years. When he began having it again, he discovered he could turn the dream's familiarity into a trigger for lucidity. He was then able to complete the dream and understand its message.

Mansion in the Forest

I am in an enormous mansion in the middle of a huge forest; it is totally isolated, with no roads or paths leading to it. It is uninhabited, with virtually no furniture. There are terazzo floors throughout, giant marble columns, huge ceilings, and windows that run around the perimeter of the walls and ceilings. The windows are circular and are set in walls that are at least a foot thick.

I am inside and desperately need to get out. I don't know why but I know I have to get away from the ground level to be safe. I feel like a bird trapped in a house and trying to find an exit, going from window to window looking for one that's open. And that's what I do, I fly forty or fifty feet up in the air, like I'm swimming underwater, and keep trying all the windows, looking for one through which I can get out. My heart is pounding, I know I have to get out to be truly safe, and yet I can't find a window that will open.

Suddenly I realize I've been here before; this is my recurrent dream. I'm still terrified and keep saying to myself, "Am I going to make it?" I'm exerting a lot of effort to stay airborne and don't know how much longer I can continue. I get angry;

I'm tired of this dream and I want to find a way out.

I decide to approach one last window; this is it, I'm getting out of here. I'm exhausted, but I use everything I have to resolutely face that window. With all my energy I stare at the window, and in my mind I order it, "You will open up for me." I stare at it as hard as I can. The window glass shimmers and gets clearer and clearer, so that the sunny forest outside becomes increasingly, almost blindingly, bright. And then I see that there is no glass; the colors are so bright because the window is open and there is just pure, clean air. I have been so mesmerized by the vividness of the scene that I have forgotten, for a moment, that I have to get out. I fly out into the air that smells of clover and honeysuckle.

In associating to the dream, the dreamer reported that the mansion reminded him of the Italianate villa built by the founders of Phillips Petroleum in Tulsa, Oklahoma, where he grew up. It was situated in the woods, with a lot of marble and statuary from abroad, and had hanging gardens in the back. There were carved staircases, a ballroom, and balconies and terraces. The villa had been donated to the city by Wade Phillips to house a museum collection, and the dreamer had often gone there, as a child, on Sunday afternoons and spent hours wandering around. The mansion in his dreams was the same style, and the woodsy setting was similar except that in his dream there were no roads, gates, or other houses. His feelings when he visited the Phillips villa were of "exploration, wanting to stay, wanting to belong, and yet also feeling frightened off because it wasn't time for me to be there."

Reflecting on this, he saw in himself a tendency to get embroiled in living, working, and personal situations that superficially or initially seemed appealing or "right," but for which he could never maintain his enthusiasm. He saw that a lot of these involvements were an attempt to fulfill his parents' and, in a larger sense, society's expectations of him, because he wanted to be accepted. He believed his dream symbolized his feeling of being trapped into living his life in a way that would please others. By working the dream through and understanding its message, he never had it again.

Analyzing the way you think: Being aware of your thought processes and questioning yourself during a dream can also result in lucidity. A particular image or situation can prompt you to ask yourself, "Where did you come from?" and in answering that question you may realize that you're dreaming. This occurred in the following dream:

The Last Kiss

I enter the room of a friend who has recently died. He's still there. He had been smoking a cigarette when he died. He is dead in the room, sitting in a chair, but the cigarette is still burning. He has been dead for three weeks and the smoke from the cigarette is billowing into the room. I feel as if there could suddenly be a big fire. I think, "Why is he still here?" Then I am with him. He is dead. I hold him in my arms and hug him. He is very thin, the way he was when he died. He reaches toward me and kisses me lovingly on the mouth. The idea that my friend is still alive though he has actually died in the physical world makes me aware that I am dreaming.

Flying dreams: A common phenomenon in both lucid and prelucid dreams is flying; many people consider it to be one of the most thrilling dream experiences. It's also a way to escape danger.

There are many variations of dream flying. Some people glide through the air with their arms outstretched; others flap their arms like birds or use swimming motions. For certain dreamers flying is effortless and they feel they can go on forever, but others find it physically exhausting and can do it for only short periods of time.

An individual's flying ability can alter over the course of his life. One dreamer reported that she had wonderful flying dreams when she was a small child. She would go up very high and fly great distances over a lush, verdant forest, swooping and soaring in and out of the branches of the trees and sometimes landing on a branch like a bird. It was an effortless, gliding sensation that she described as "pure pleasure."

As she entered her mid-teens it become more difficult for her to fly and she had fewer flying dreams. Those that she did have were fights for survival from faceless danger; her heart would be pounding and her pulse would race, and she would be terrified that she wasn't going to make it. Her method of flying also changed, and she had to use a strenuous, underwater-swimming motion to become airborne and attain height. She recalled that as her flying ability diminished, she felt a deep, though inarticulated, sense of loss, wistfulness, and melancholy; it was as if her childhood were gone and she knew she'd never experience it again.

However, during a period in her late teens when things were going well for her and she was pleased with where she was, she suddenly started having pleasurable flying dreams again. She reports that she hasn't had flying dreams for a long time, but has had them as an adult. She believes they're tied in with a sense of freedom, limitless options, and not being burdened down with the minutiae of day-to-day life and responsibility.

EXERCISE 24

Learn to Fly in Your Dream

If you don't currently fly in your dreams, it's possible to teach yourself to do it. Before you go to sleep, think about flying. Select a flying method and visualize yourself flying in your dreams. Imagine the sensations you would have if you were flying. Repeat to yourself, "I am going to fly in my dreams." If you awaken during the night, remind yourself that you want to fly and picture yourself doing it.

This dreamer taught herself to fly, and it became an important symbol, in both her waking and dream life, for success and accomplishment.

Entertaining the Family

I enter a big country chateau; it's a private family home donated to become a Jewish family center. Different functions are held there. I am there to do leaded glass work and am supposed to take preliminary measurements. I'm alarmed to hear voices. I peek in and am surprised to see the owner of the house, who is a friend, with a group of women. I am more surprised to see my friend than to see the women. My friend does not look happy; she is surrounded by family-type people. It looks like she's having to run a wedding shower all by herself. People have brought gifts and there is colored wrapping paper strewn around. She is fooling around with a tray of food and has to make sure everyone is served; she's in charge of a lot of things. When we see each other, I have the feeling that I'm intruding. Usually when we see each other it's for social, good times, but now she's involved in business. I tell her I'm there to do these measurements, but she doesn't know how to explain me to her family. And so I say, "Don't be worried. Tell them I'm here to entertain. I'll show them how I can fly. And you can say, 'A friend dropped in.'"

But then I add, "I'm not sure this can work, I can't always do this. I may flop and I may drop into the buffet. There are gifts and these people's heads, and if I fly low there could be an accident." But my friend wants me to do it, and I say I'll try. I put my hands out in front of me, sort of like Superman, and tuck my head in a little to streamline myself for my takeoff position. I have to start at an angle and go forward gradually; I can't shoot straight up like a missile. My friend looks worried and I think, "Oh God, if I don't do this I'm going to be in hot water." But I manage to get up there, so I fly around awhile and show off. Everyone is astonished and happy to see such a feat. The top of the house looks like a cathedral; there are dark beams. It's not very bright and it isn't easy to fly. There isn't much space and I have to be careful not to fly into the beams. I land back down on the carpeted floor and there is a feeling of relief.

The dreamer saw much of her current life reflected in this dream. She is swamped with projects, one of which is working under enormous pressure to complete a stained glass window of a Shalom lithograph on time for a show at the New York Coliseum. Shalom of Safed is one of the twentieth century's foremost primitive artists. He's Jewish, and she associated the Jewish family center in the dream with the fact that she's trying to prove she can do a Jewish work of art even though she's not Jewish. The window entails meticulous work; it's on a different scale from the etching and requires, among other things, cutting very tiny pieces of glass. The dreamer says she often feels as if she's flying when she works on the piece. If she accomplishes it on time, which she isn't sure she can do, she will "fly high." She later reported, after the piece had been finished on time, that she does indeed feel as if she's flying.

Flying in your dreams is not only fun and exciting, but it can also transport you into a lucid dream state. Once there, you have the power to accomplish many things. You may, for example, prolong these pleasurable aspects of your dream; you may discover the solutions to your problems—personal, creative, or otherwise. Some of these solutions may result from examining the underlying dynamics of your fears. Others may come from simply coping with difficult feelings rather than running away from them. The courage and knowledge you gain in your lucid dreams can carry over into your waking life.

13

Decoding Your Nightmares

You are being chased by an object of unspeakable horror; every facet of annihilation is encompassed in its form. And yet your legs can move only in slow motion; it takes unbearably long to take a single step, and your frantic struggle to run faster is futile. Your pursuer looms inexorably closer and desperation becomes terror. You know you're not going to escape. You can't breathe, and hysterically gulp for air that isn't there. You are totally helpless, eye to eye with the instrument of your impending death.

Then you wake up, gasping for air, heart pounding, face wet with tears and cold sweat. It takes a few moments for you to reorient yourself to reality and relax, for your heart and breathing to slow down. Most of you will then thank God it was "just a dream" and go back to sleep. But for some people, the terror they've experienced makes them afraid to sleep, and this secondary fear can lead to insomnia and irritability.

Most of us, fortunately, don't respond quite so severely, but nightmares and other bad dreams can still be traumatic experiences. Sleep is a private, vulnerable time, and a nightmare can feel like an evil intruder violating us. But nightmares can also be viewed, and used, as positive experiences; what we feel has invaded us is really a part of ourselves fighting to come out. Nightmares can be catalysts for forcing us to recognize feelings that desperately need our attention, and can spotlight which of our many emotional needs should be a priority at that time. Dreamwork can be enormously helpful in decoding these dreams and providing access to the important insights struggling to reach our consciousness. All of the dreamwork exercises offered in this book can be helpful with nightmares, but the ones presented in this chapter are especially effective.

Background

For centuries, nightmares were thought to be evil spirits who inhabited the soul when the person was asleep. After all, what kind of human mind could, and would, conjure up such visions of horror? No one wanted to take responsibility for such thoughts. Strangely enough, despite scientific and psychological revelations, nightmares continue to be tied to the mystical. In *Webster's Third New International Dictionary* the first of the definitions of "nightmare" is: "An evil spirit formerly thought to oppress people during sleep: as a. INCUBUS [evil spirit that has sex with women while they are asleep]* b. SUCCUBUS [evil spirit that has sex with men while they're asleep] c. A hag sometimes believed to be accompanied by nine attendant spirits...."[1] The idea of a specific evil spirit that causes dreams of terror goes back at least as far as the tenth century in Western European culture[2] and I think it's safe to assume that similar beliefs predate that time in most cultures. This spirit was known as a *mare* in Old and Middle English (thus the word *nightmare*); a similar concept was evident in the Old High German and Old Norse word *mara*, meaning incubus.[3]

As you can see, Freud was by no means the first to ascribe sexual conflict to nightmares; the sexuality of the spirit *mare* is one of its primary distinguishing characteristics. Freud's biographer, Ernest Jones, noted that Freud, in a sense, retained the image of the evil spirit but renamed it *libido.* According to Freud, every dream represents the fulfillment of a repressed wish. When the nature of the wish is extremely unacceptable (sexual, especially incestuous) and yet the force of the desire threatens to overcome the repression, a nightmare occurs and the conflict is interrupted by the dreamer's waking up.[4] A Freudian interpretation of a nightmare may point out forbidden feelings and neuroses, but simply knowing these feelings, in my opinion, will not automatically bring a healing. You can intellectually understand the meaning of a dream and still feel miserable.

Carl Jung believed dream characters were all different aspects of ourselves. Fritz Perls borrowed Jung's idea and used it in conjunction with his own theories to help patients bring forth the missing parts of their personali-

---

*Bracketed material mine.

ties and then reenact them, in order to form the true gestalt, or totality.

Jung originated the important concept of the "shadow"—an undesirable, often threatening dream character of the same sex as the dreamer. Sometimes portrayed as a madman, beggar, or assassin, the "shadow" is a part of ourself that we deny and repress; it will continue to torment us until it is recognized and integrated into our consciousness. Once brought out, however, this aspect of ourself will often turn out also to have positive qualities that enhance our total personality and being.

The psychologist Calvin Hall viewed nightmares as self-punishment for disregarding certain tenets of the conscience and yielding to temptation. The nightmare indicated the price the dreamer thought he would have to pay for his transgression.[5]

Nightmares and bad dreams occupy a substantial portion of our dream life. Calvin Hall made a study of ten thousand dreams that revealed that sixty-four percent were associated with apprehension, anger, and sadness, and that only eighteen percent were happy or exciting. Hostile acts by or against the dreamer (murder, physical attack, denunciation) outnumbered friendly ones more than two to one.

Night terrors, nightmares, and bad dreams

For the purposes of clarification, it's helpful to separate night terrors, nightmares, and bad dreams into their primary categories:

Night terrors (pavor nocturnus) are a sleep disorder similar to nightmares that occurs primarily in children. Unlike nightmares, they occur during the early, non-REM part of the sleep cycle. Night terrors are very brief, usually lasting only a minute or two, and are composed of a single, uncontrollable, terrifying scene. The child awakes screaming in terror and has a hard time getting rid of his fear, but has no memory of the dream content.[6] Most children plagued by night terrors eventually outgrow them; this leads some doctors to suggest they're due to delayed central-nervous-system maturation.[7] Freud believed night terrors were sexual impulses that had not been understood and thus had been repudiated. He thought they were brought on by accidental, exciting impressions and successive waves of spontaneous developmental processes.[8]

Nightmares are severe anxiety dreams where the fear and the issues in the dream are so intense that they wake up the dreamer. They occur during regular REM sleep, usually last fifteen to twenty minutes,[9] and are often complex compilations of scenes than can be remembered in great detail. Many people have recurring themes and actions in their nightmares; common ones are: paralysis, suffocation, falling, drowning, death, being nude in public, wandering on a lonely road, being chased or followed, trying to get someplace and not being able to find the road, not being able to lock doors against an intruder, not being able to open doors when being chased, having to take an exam in a subject you've never studied, being an actor on stage and not knowing your lines.

Many people have what seems to be *warning dreams* of impending disaster, usually the death of someone they know. In the great majority of cases the catastrophe never occurs, and another explanation can be found for the dream. However, there are those who report being able to predict future events from their dreams; through enough dream experience you may learn to determine the degree of your ESP-type powers. Your dreams can also warn you about the state of your physical health. From Galen and Hippocrates, the fathers of modern medicine, to Freud and Jung, to modern-day doctors like Dr. Bernard Siegal, dreams have been valued as diagnostic tools. Dr. Siegal writes, "There is an intimate relationship between psyche and soma. When something goes wrong, even if it's in your big toe, your mind knows it."[10] He has found numerous instances where dreams predicted physical illnesses before the conventional medical tests did.[11]

Usually illness dreams are cloaked in metaphor. Jung noted that animals are often used to represent the physical self; houses are another common image for the body. The dreamworker Jeremy Taylor notices that "dreams of broken furnaces often presage bouts of gastrointestinal distress; dreams of faulty wiring and plumbing often have reference to disorders of nerves, emotions, and sexual life."[12] The dream researcher Meredith Sabini found that cars were frequently used to represent the body, with the headlights corresponding to eyes, the four tires to the four limbs, the electrical system to the nervous system, etc.[13] Warning dreams of physical illnesses are not always disguised. If you have recurring anxiety dreams concerning a part of your body, you might consider visiting your doctor.

Another category of bad dreams is the *guilt dream*. Here the dreamer is not the victim (as is customary in nightmares and bad dreams) but rather is the murderer or the one who has hurt someone else, and not in self-defense. The dream expresses all the guilt the dreamer is repressing, and dreamwork can help identify its source.

Anxiety dreams are similar to nightmares in their themes and feelings of fear but are not as intense and do not cause the dreamer to awaken in fright. These dreams can be very disturbing, whether or not they're remembered, because the feelings of anxiety and fear can linger even when the person doesn't recall what evoked them.

Beyond your fear

Daniel Berlin aptly wrote regarding nightmares, "At the place of our greatest fear lies our power."[14] Dreams provide the ideal arena in which to work past fear because they are ultimately safe; we can't be physically harmed, and our psyches prevent us from delving deeper into a dream than we can handle. However, experiencing our fear in our dreams can enable us to become more fearless in our waking life.

An interesting difference between waking life fear and dream fear is that in waking life we escape it by figuratively going to sleep (repressing and blocking our feelings), and in dream life we escape fear by waking up. A key part of working with nightmares, though, is learning *not* to wake up; unless we confront our demons and complete the experience, they can come back to haunt us. As Fritz Perls writes, "When we accept and *enter* this nothingness, the void, then the desert starts to bloom. The empty void becomes alive, is being filled, the sterile void becomes the fertile void."[15] The following are exercises and suggestions for going into and beyond your fear so that you can attain the power that is rightfully and inherently yours.

Lucid dreaming and dream reentry

One of the best ways to deal with nightmares is to turn them into lucid dreams; that is, to become aware that you're dreaming while in the dream state. There are several ways to train yourself to lucid dream, and I elaborated on them in the previous chapter. I want to emphasize here their invaluable help in enabling the dreamer to confront his dream enemies and complete or change the frightening dream experience, instead of awaking in terror. In a lucid dream, you know that no harm will come to you in a dangerous situation, but that doesn't mean you don't experience the fear. Instead, knowing that it isn't "real" allows you to stay with the situation and feel the terror instead of running away. Learning how to cope with fear in your dream life can teach you how to handle it better in your waking life.

EXERCISE 25

Reenter Your Dream

Until you have learned to dream lucidly, the technique we have described as dream reentry can serve you in much the same way while you're in a waking state. If the nightmare has awakened you, you can go back into it as if you are still dreaming it; you then have the power to do anything you want with the dream, including changing it to a pleasurable one. Practicing the reentry exercise facilitates the ability to dream lucidly since it uses the same dream skills.

A young actor reported starting out a night's dream journey with the following nightmare.

The Airplane

I'm in a small plane, flying over the Pacific Ocean. I fly down close to the water and see a Boeing 747 floating in the ocean, not far from shore. Somehow I get the news that there's been an accident and everyone is dead. I learn that the pilot thought he had landed in Santa Monica, on the airport runway. The stewardesses had then gone below to open up the baggage compartment and, since they were on water, this had caused an explosion that killed everyone without destroying anything. The effect is as if the plane had plummeted hundreds of feet down into the ocean, even though in reality it is floating on the surface. I fly down closer, and suddenly I'm in the water, swimming around the plane as I examine it. Dead, bloated bodies float all around me. It's clear death occurred instantly since all the corpses have relaxed, smiling expressions; they never knew what happened. It's very quiet; I'm the only living person. I'm surprised that none of the bodies appear injured, and the plane itself is in perfect condition. I become terrified as I realize I could have easily made the same mistake. I wonder how this could have happened; why didn't the stewardesses or one of the passengers look out the window and see that they were still on water? My fear for my own safety grows; I'm convinced I can't stop myself from doing the same thing. More hideous, grinning bodies float around me. I wake up out of terror.

The dreamer awoke with a vivid recollection of the dream, and decided to reenter it. Still half-asleep, he moved back into the position he'd been in when he awakened; he successfully stepped back into the dream and continued it in this way.

The Airplane (Reentered)

I paddle around in the water, and the grotesque, bloated bodies surround me. I feel like I'm going to vomit, and I act out my fear and revulsion; my face twists in agony. The moment, and the scene, freeze for a second as I peak at the zenith of my torment. Climax reached, I decide to change the dream. The corpses become plastic balloons with faces painted on them, like children's punching bags. I raise my right arm into the air like Superman and fly straight up out of the water and land on a nearby pier. Steven Spielberg [the film director] is there, along with cameras and a whole movie crew. We're shooting an expensive comedy movie, and we've just done a perfect first take of an elaborate scene.

Everyone is in a good, lighthearted mood; Spielberg puts his arm around me and tells me what a great actor I am, how realistic and dramatic my expressions were. I sheepishly confess that I had forgotten it was just a movie while we were filming the scene, and he tells me that's great, the way it should be, to get a good performance. He informs me we have to shoot the scene one more time, for coverage, and I walk off to my trailer to get dry and made-up to do the scene again. I feel very confident and happy.

In this case the dreamer went back into the nightmare and let himself feel the full extent of his terror and then, as a reward for going all the way with it, used his imagination not only to lift himself out of the nightmare but also to put himself into one of his greatest real-life dreams—a starring role in a major Hollywood movie. He was thus able to turn his terror into pleasure. This dream experience also provided him with some insight into his anxiety regarding his precarious acting career. He saw the downed plane and the grotesque corpses as all the struggling actors who never make it, and felt his fear and self-loathing at the idea that he could be one of them. But through his dream he learned that experiencing his fears at their most intense level can be more than just acceptable, it can be *good*, for it can give him added depth and dimension in his craft, and thus increase his chance for success.

A patient used the reentry exercise during a crucial period in her life. The dreamwork she did was a turning point in her therapy and enabled her to attain a dramatic new level of personality integration. This was her dream.

The Scream

The young man is bitten by a rattlesnake as he stands in a pond of water. He dies. I'm watching with a crowd of people. The most horrifying part is the scream when he is bitten. He had been bitten once before but it was just a little twinge—and he knew he'd be bitten again. When the rattlesnake bites him again, it sinks both fangs into the instep of his left foot. Blood comes out in the shape of the rattlesnake; it is fanned at the top the way a cobra becomes when it's about to bite somebody. The horrifying part is that he stands there letting out these screams that just fill the air over the pond and fill the sky.

The day following the dream, the image of the man screaming kept coming to my patient's mind. "I couldn't push it away," she reported, "so I faced up to it. I went back into the dream. The experience was very much like what I experience when I'm here and I face something I don't want to. The scream was the scream of all the pain in this man's life . . . all the regrets, all the remorse. It was a scream of battle. It was a scream of defeat. And it was a scream of death, because he was dying. It was the scream and the expression on his face that I had to confront. I kept making myself see that face and hear the scream. I kept saying out loud, 'Who is he? Who is he?' until I said, 'That's you and your death and that's your pain.' And the more I faced up to that, the more I would cry. I began crying and crying and moaning and howling until all the horror I felt from the dream went away. And then I was able to accept its message and that I had dreamed it."

As the patient was reexamining the dream, her mind presented an image of a face from a painting called "Childhood." "This painting," the patient said, "showed the various stages of childhood and children's faces, some not formed. And some don't have eyes—just sockets, and their mouths open in horror as they enter the adult world. The man's face in the dream was a screaming skull. Each time I connected to the origin of that image, I cried again." At the end of the session, the patient remarked, "Sometimes I still experience the anxieties that I came here with, the helplessness, that lost feeling—but with one change. I am aware that *I* am doing it. And I can then change what I'm doing. Also, I've started to see myself as a pretty person, and not afraid of being attractive to anyone. Since I don't feel ugly anymore, I'm able to look at people on the street and not be afraid they'll look at me. I'm not worried about what I am, who I am."

Since the beginning of therapy, this patient had been combining talking with drawing during her sessions. Up till this point, her drawing had shown great disorganization and fragmentation. But her drawing during this session was markedly different. There was harmony and integration in the drawing she made of a flower that filled the page; she drew each petal from the center of the flower. This drawing resembled the lotus of countless petals which is equivalent to the third eye, the opening of higher consciousness.

Triumph over your demons

The essential message of this chapter is that nightmares are a blessing in disguise, because through them we can experience and conquer fear. Once a dreamer learns to fight and triumph over his demons, they lose their power to frighten. This approach is a fundamental part of the Senoi people's dream philosophy, and is enormously helpful with nightmares.

The philosopher and biographer Leon Edel noted that Henry James, author of the classic ghost tale *The Turn of the Screw*, used this exercise with his frequent nightmares: "[Henry James] recorded in his autobiographies the memory of a nightmare which he described as 'appalling' while at the same time calling it 'admirable' and a 'dream-adventure.' Fear and delight were mingled in it. He dreamed that he was defending himself in abject terror against an invader, fighting to keep him from bursting through the closed door of his room. Then suddenly the tables were turned. The door was open. However, instead of the monster entering he saw that it was racing down a great corridor filled with works of art amid thunder and lightning. He recognized the place: it was the grand Galerie d'Apollon in the Louvre. What had begun as a nightmare of confrontation ended in total victory.... Henry James seemed to be saying with Dr. Johnson, 'I, sir, should have frightened the ghost.' ... [This dream] suggests that he discovered in some strange way the means by which he could both dream of terror and find the control and defense to banish it. He seems to have had to fight this kind of battle repeatedly, for there are records of other and similar dreams with this recurrent theme."[16]

Triumphing over your demons can be used in both lucid dreams and in dream reentry; often just consciously deciding to do this implants the victory in your unconscious. An elderly man successfully used this exercise on this recurring nightmare:

Street Gang

I am walking alone, on a dark city street. Suddenly
I meet up with an ominous group of young, tough
men and women. They chase me down the street,
trying to kill me.

At this point, the dreamer always awoke in fear. He
finally decided he was tired of being chased by this same
group of thugs night after night, and told himself as he
went back to sleep that he was going to get his friends
and go back to the gang and fight them. That firm resolution led him to have the following lucid dream.

Street Gang (A Lucid Dream)

My friends and I walk along a devastated city
street; it's either the day after a nuclear bomb
attack or we're in the South Bronx. We're all
dressed in black jumpsuits; they're terrorist-
fighting uniforms. We meet up with the gang;
they're murderously threatening and my friends
and I wordlessly turn and start to flee. Then I decide it's very wrong for us to run; we *must* fight
them instead. The others seem to instantly realize
the same thing, for we all stop and turn around at
the same time. We stand close together and march
toward the gang. Where before we were frightened
individuals, we are now a strong, solid, purposeful
mass. We head ominously toward the gang and
they increase their threats but don't touch us; we
are silent and invincible. We mow down the thugs
like a bulldozer; they hit us and wave knives but
we are a block of granite and don't feel a thing. We
leave them squashed flat on the sidewalk, like in a
cartoon, and move off to reclaim our city.

The dreamer reported sleeping very deeply and peacefully after that dream, the most satisfying sleep he'd had in weeks. He said he awoke with a great sense of accomplishment and strength, and now declares, "I dare my demons to come back to my door." So far, none have returned.

E X E R C I S E 2 6

Become Friends with Your Foes

It's not always necessary to fight your scary dream images. You will find that if you confront some of these frightening figures and ask them what they want, they cease to be threatening and instead become dream friends. A dreamer who has taught himself to complete his nightmares instead of awaken from them, reported that this dream started out as a nightmare but became wonderfully exciting when he confronted what he thought were his foes:

The UFO

I'm in my home town. A huge UFO is traveling overhead; it's pretty crude-looking, like a Jules Verne creation. As it moves overhead it sucks up everything in its path—people, houses, cars, etc. —like an enormous vacuum cleaner. The special effects are terrific, like a *Star Wars* movie, but it's very frightening. I'm in a house with a lot of people; it feels like a family reunion. Everyone is frantic, running around the house crying and screaming, trying to figure out what it will suck up next. There's total chaos; it's like the Final Holocaust. Everyone runs from room to room, window to window, trying to figure out if and when it will get us. Suddenly I hear my mother call me from another room. "Come here, they're setting the neighbor's house on fire!"

I want to flee all this by waking, and feel myself on the verge of doing so, but instead decide to go on with the dream and allow myself to be sucked up. I see the shadow on the spaceship moving across the lawn toward the house, and I stiffen in anticipation. Then I feel my hair stand straight up as if it's being tugged by a gentle, invisible force. Suddenly I'm outside, flying straight up as I'm sucked up into the spaceship. Though I'm moving very fast, it's a surprisingly fun, unfrightening sensation.

Then I'm in the spaceship with one of the aliens. It's not at all human-looking and yet I'm not surprised or repelled; it's as if I subconsciously knew they would look like this. The alien speaks first, "We didn't set that house on fire. The people inside must have done that. We're not doing that." I ask it what they are doing and what they want. I'm surprised at how calm I feel and how rational everything seems. The alien is amazed that I don't know. "Why, we're embracing you, making love to you. We unite with you so that both of us can fully know the other." I ask what happens afterward, and the alien points out the back window of the spaceship; in its trail are the people, houses, etc., floating back down to earth. It's beautiful, like something out of Walt Disney's *Fantasia*. There's celestial music. Even though I'm so far up, I can see the blissful look on the people's faces. I turn to the alien and say, "Yes, but look at the people ahead of you. They're terrified; they don't know that you're not going to hurt them. You shouldn't do this without their permission." The alien is very apologetic; it never occurred to these space people that we might be frightened because they don't know how to be anything but loving and protective. It's just taken for granted that all interaction is friendly and pleasurable. I'm touched by its sincerity; it's a sweet, innocent creature that only knows love. The alien orders the crew to stop the spaceship and let the last people down. It asks what to do next, and I say they should wait for the people who have met them to tell the ones who haven't about the experience, and let them choose whether they want to do it. I really like this creature and offer to be a go-between. It asks if I want to go through the embrace; I feel kind of shy but say yes. We shake hands, and the alien seems like a brother. It says they will always be there for me. Then the alien directs me to a door.

I feel a little scared as I start to open the door and wonder for a second if I've been tricked, but when I pass through it I am enraptured. It seems like I'm floating in gold air. There's no one else there, but I feel enveloped by a wondrous presence. I start feeling all kinds of incredibly pleasurable physical sensations. It's both sexual and beyond sexual; I'm feeling things I never knew existed; and it's fabulous beyond words.

The dreamer said he awoke the next morning feeling terrific, and called this nightmare his best dream ever. These aliens have become his dream friends, and he says he's called on them to rescue him from other nightmares.

This exercise is also based in Senoi dream theory, and the practice they've found useful: asking the new dream friend for a gift. What you get may surprise you, and give you more insight about your needs and desires.

The Senoi also believe in calling upon dream friends when in dire need of help. A woman successfully used the Senoi practice with her youngest daughter. The girl was plagued by recurring nightmares of a sea monster coming out of the ocean toward her, and would always awaken in terror. The mother told the girl that the next time the monster appeared, she should call upon Jodie for help; Jodie was a friend of the girl's older sister and the child greatly admired her. The next time the young girl dreamed of the sea monster, she called to Jodie. Jodie appeared, the sea monster shriveled up into a little rubber toy, and the nightmare disappeared forever.

E X E R C I S E   2 7

Rewrite Your Dream from the Other Character's Point of View

A well-known axiom of war is "Know your enemy," and it's pertinent to your battles with dream enemies, too, especially since some of them might be parts of yourself. Aside from having a dialogue with these characters, you can get to know them better by rewriting the dream from their point of view. Unlike previous exercises involving a dialogue or becoming everything in your dream, this exercise affords you the added dimension of understanding how your antagonist views you and the world. The exercise can be of enormous help in understanding a contrary opinion and not contaminating it with your own. In essence, it is allowing the hidden part of yourself that is critical or threatening to express itself full force while your conscious ego listens undefended. When you start this exercise you may have no idea who these dream characters are. But just by virtue of telling their story of the dream, their true intentions and identities will emerge.

A woman found this exercise invaluable with this nightmare:

Evil Woman

I'm on Fifth Avenue in New York. Among all the traffic are two people in costume, on stilts. I realize they're dressed up as Jesus and Mary, and that both of them are women.

Then I'm in my loft, only it's on a different street. The huge loft occupies the first and second floors of the building. There are two aluminum and glass doors between the loft and the street. Three women come by; two of them are the ones who were dressed as Jesus and Mary, but they're no longer in costume. They open the outside door. As I go to meet them I realize the inside door isn't locked either. They ask me where a particular man lives. Though I act friendly, I really want to get rid of them. I tell them I don't know the man and suggest they look up his address in the phone book in the booth at the corner. I say that, not even knowing if there is a phone booth there. I realize it's not safe to have the doors unlocked, so I jiggle the latches of both doors to make sure they're locked. But before I have a chance to lock them, one of the three women returns. She opens both doors and enters my loft. She looks around and says, "You have a lot of space for just one person. It looks like you have a lot of valuable things." I get very scared, and decide to tell her I have a few room-mates, and that some of them are upstairs and the others will be home soon. Before I get a chance to say this, she menacingly walks into the room, toward me. I'm terrified that she has a gun, and start yelling for help. I'm shouting in real life, and my screams awaken my boyfriend sleeping next to me. He wakes me up and tells me that I'm dreaming.

This was the first time the dreamer ever recalled shouting for help in her sleep, and she wanted to know more about this dream character who was threatening her. She rewrote the dream from the evil woman's point of view.

Evil Woman (Woman's Point of View)

I'm walking down Fifth Avenue with my friend. There are cars stuck in traffic jams all around us; it's unbelievably noisy, filthy, and disgusting. My friend and I are protected from this by our Jesus and Mary costumes, and our stilts enable us to see right over everyone else. Everyone notices us, they can't help but notice us; we're colorful, dazzling, special, so different from all of them. We go down, down, down Fifth Avenue. I love being so different from all the gray, noisy, disgusting people.

Now we're at some huge home, opening right onto the street. Those people inside are just asking for trouble! It's so bright in there, so visible from the busy street; it's an affront to the rest of us, showing off all its space and goodies. We ask the woman in there how to find the man and she acts very superior, telling us to get lost and go find a phone. We don't need her. I hate being put off by condescending people like her. Who does she think she is? Bragging and putting us down, that's all her big loft is. I'll get her. But it will be smooth, she won't have a chance against me.

Now I'm alone. I don't need those people I was with, I can get her on my own, by myself. If I need the others to help, they'll be back later. I try the doors and they're unlocked, both of them. What an idiot! She's really asking for it. She has to let me in because she likes to seem friendly. But she's not friendly, she's nothing. I'll get her good. I have the gun if I need it but I bet I won't; she'll let me just walk right in and take over the place. She'll wish she had never met me.

The dreamer said that when she first began writing the exercise, her initial thoughts were, "This is very revealing. This is definitely a scary person, an ominous threat." Through writing the dream from the evil woman's point of view, she was able to experience the frightening image as a part of herself. She said, "This seems like the suicidal part of myself, attacking me for being unworthy and inferior. I don't deserve what I have and thus will lose it." I asked her why she had let the danger, the evil woman, into her loft, and her instant reply was, "Because I wanted her to like me." The dreamer then said that her mother had always made her feel inferior and unworthy in subtle ways. Though her mother had never expressed her anger overtly, the dreamer had always sensed it was there; she felt criticized and undermined without knowing why. She had continued trying to win her mother's approval and affection even after her mother had hurt her. She had always felt that if she got angry and turned away from her mother, her mother would irrevocably leave her; and so she had to make her mother like her, no matter how angry or hurt she felt. Her anger toward her mother was then turned and directed at herself.

Through doing this exercise, the dreamer gained a clearer understanding about an aspect of herself that Jung termed the "shadow"—an undesirable trait that she didn't want to acknowledge. She came to understand her mother's subtle sabotage, and saw that the evil woman represented not only the dreamer herself, but also an aspect of her mother as well, whom she had allowed to "just walk right in and take over." Recognizing and admitting these feelings, and understanding their source, helped to defuse some of their destructive power over her.

Rewriting a dream from the other character's point of view can also be useful when this character is an identifiable person in our waking life. We are often so wrapped up in our own feelings that we have a hard time seeing what's going on inside others. Rewriting the dream from their point of view enables us to feel their emotions without being blocked or distracted by our own.

A woman had this nightmare during a difficult period in her therapy. A lot of painful, buried feelings were being stirred up, and she was especially sensitive about her newly recognized feelings of needfulness. She felt more fragmented and vulnerable than she had in a long time, and she knew the feeling was due to the therapy. During the day preceding this dream, she had had a particularly difficult session with the therapist. In a lot of pain, she asked the therapist to treat her as a human being for a moment instead of a patient, and to give her a comforting hug. The therapist refused, and the dreamer left the session feeling hurt, angry, and rejected. That night she had this nightmare:

Swimming in Black

I am swimming in a black ocean at night. There's no moon or stars, nothing but black water and black air. I'm not alone; I know there's a woman in a boat near me. I can't see her but I'm positive she's there. At first I'm OK; I'm confident I'm heading for shore. But as I grow tired, I get scared because I still can't see the shore. I realize I'll never be able to see the shore because it's too dark. I start to doubt my sense of direction; maybe I've taken a wrong turn and I'm not even heading for it. I stop swimming and look all around me; the black is so flat and total that it feels like it's smothering me. I want to start swimming again, desperate to escape this black, but I don't remember which way I was heading. I don't know if that way is the right way, but it's the only way I know. Lost and confused, my energy drains out of me. The water becomes rough and the waves pull me under. I realize I'm going to drown and become frantic. I remember the woman in the boat and call out to her. I still can't see her, but she calmly and matter-of-factly tells me I'm drowning. She goes into minute detail describing all my physical sensations and my growing panic. She knows everything I'm experiencing, as if she had X-ray vision into me. And yet she makes no effort to rescue me or tell me where she is. What the hell's wrong with her! I don't need to know how I feel, I need the God-damn boat! I frantically swim around trying to find her and grab onto the boat. I flounder about in the water, pathetically, desperately reaching out in every direction. My grasping hands claw at the water and air; there's nothing solid like flesh or wood. The woman continues to itemize all the nuances of my terror; her quiet, controlled voice seems louder than my screams for help. Though she knows my anguish as intimately as I do, she's completely unaffected by it. God damn her! I trusted her! My effort to find her exhausts me; it's hopeless so I gave up my search. She dispassionately narrates my impending death and I stop swimming. I wake up.

The dreamer awoke from the nightmare sobbing with terror, and it left her feeling even more miserable. The dream corroborated her feelings that the therapist, having upset her by putting her in touch with disturbing emotions, was now going to abandon her to her pain and confusion. She felt hopeless and depressed. I suggested that she rewrite the dream from the point of view of her therapist.

Swimming in Black (Therapist's Point of View)

I am in a boat, watching the young woman swim. It's ironic; I know she feels she's in total darkness, and yet I see her magnified under bright light. I watch her carefully; I am with her every second, feeling all her emotions, knowing all her thoughts. It's OK that she can't see me; it's enough that I can see her. She becomes tired and confused. Her arms flail around, like an infant's or a blind person's, trying to grab hold of me. I want to reach out and rescue her but I can't. I'm in another dimension, so close that I'm inside her and yet too far for there to be any crossover of our worlds. I talk to her, tell her I know what she's feeling, and hope she'll realize that she has grabbed hold of me. She doesn't feel me. I probe deeper, exploring all her vulnerabilities in an effort to get in and reach her. I try to compensate for the limitations, both in myself and intrinsic to the situation, by going as far as I can in the ways that I can. I wish she'd hurry up and get it; sharing her terror becomes overwhelming at times. I don't know what else I can do. God damn it, girl, stop looking for me! You have me, as much as you can. I think (and pray) it's as much as you need. The way to save yourself is not to hold on to me; you have to fly!

This experience proved to be both emotional and revelatory for the dreamer. She cried as she realized that the woman, her therapist, was trying to save her in the best way she could. Through experiencing her therapist's concern, she felt much more secure that her therapist wouldn't abandon her or let her become uncontrollably crazy. It was crucial that this trust be cemented at this point in her therapy. Thus this nightmare, which began as such a destructive experience, became the catalyst for a positive, soothing insight.

EXERCISE 28

Have a Dialogue with the Major Emotion in Your Dream

One positive aspect of nightmares and bad dreams is their ability to keep us honest with ourselves; they prevent us from ignoring the things we intuitively know but don't want to be true. We all have an inner guide that can't be conned and that will, if more subtle forms of communication fail, scare us half to death to get our attention. A good way to determine the cause of your inner guide's concern is to have a dialogue with the major emotion in the dream. Behind the fear is its reason, and it's this knowledge that your inner voice is telling you that you can't ignore.

The following is a nightmare reported by a young man who had recently moved to New York to start a new job and a new life.

The Cult

I enter a large building along with a lot of other people; we're all going to a lecture. My new friend R stands outside the building, passing out leaflets encouraging people to enter and promoting the cult that is holding the lecture. I go inside and sit in one of the seats in the auditorium; it's very crowded. We face a stage; behind it is a small swimming pool and behind that is a large pool. One by one everyone enters the small pool, as if being baptized, and then the man who appears to be the head of the cult throws them back into the large pool, as if that's part of the ceremony.

Suddenly I'm one of the many people swimming around in the big pool. We're having a great time; it's like a party. Then suddenly, from either end of the pool, emerge two thick sheets of wood. They quickly start covering the pool, like a floor, and before I know it they have almost joined in the middle. Everyone is forced underwater since there's no air space between the water and the wood. We all panic as we realize we're going to drown. I get the feeling we're going to be replaced by look-alike monsters. My last vision is of being underwater and looking up, past my air bubbles, and seeing the two sheets of wood coming together. I realize I'm going to die, and I wake up.

The dreamer's major emotion in this nightmare was his fear of drowning. He delved deeper into it by writing out this dialogue with it, and was amazed at the way his emotion immediately developed its own "voice."

The Cult (Dialogue)

I: Why are you here?

FEAR: To make you see how awful it is to drown, to be killed by your surroundings, suffocated and smothered by something incompatible with who you are.

I: What is your connection to this cult?

FEAR: They do my work for me; they provide the swimming pool and the excuse to get you in there. They can also steal your physical body. I want you to feel the horror of knowing you're dying, and yet also knowing your body will go on without you. Your body is not you.

At this point the dreamer understood his dream. His new lifestyle was much different from his previous one —more sophisticated, he thought. He was quite taken with his new friends, and with the excitement of fast-paced partying until dawn. And yet he had always retained a vague sense of discomfort. He had ignored this feeling because he didn't want it to ruin his fun, but now saw that his nightmare was telling him he couldn't ignore it any longer. His inner guide was telling him that his new image and life-style were not himself, and that he was close to losing himself to it. A strong part of him didn't want to die and was warning him by making him experience how awful losing himself would be.

The next time you have a nightmare or bad dream,

think of it as a gift rather than a curse, a challenge rather than a threat. For in that dream is the opportunity to acquire greater confidence, self-fulfillment, and wisdom.

14

Summary

*B*y now you've no doubt discovered the unique way dreamwork exercises bring important inner knowledge to the surface, where it can be understood and used in your everyday life. The following is a review of these exercises and the ways in which they work.

EXERCISE 1

Answering Key Questions

Your dream journal is a primary tool in all the dreamwork exercises; the more you're able to express in your initial written account of the dream, the more effective the other exercises will be. The seven questions given in Chapter 1 will elicit the significant details and emotions.

E X E R C I S E   2

Making a Symbol Dictionary

Each of you has a unique symbol language that expresses your hidden feelings and impulses in your dreams. This dictionary-like format makes it easy to identify these symbols and explore their meaning in subsequent dreams. Over a period of time you'll be able to chart their development and your own related personal growth.

E X E R C I S E   3

Talking with Your Symbol

Writing out a dialogue with a key symbol is a simple, direct way to get your questions answered. You'll be able to feel its "personality" and understand its consequence in your life.

E X E R C I S E   4

Translating Metaphors

Dreams often present their messages in a series of emotionally impactful metaphors. This exercise provides a framework for translating these metaphors and understanding their meanings in the context of your waking life.

EXERCISE 5

Step Back into Your Dream

Dreams can be confusing, with frightening situations and perplexing characters. Your dream partner can guide you back into the dream in a waking state so that you can explore and resolve those aspects that troubled you during your initial experience of the dream.

EXERCISE 6

Experience Your Partner's Dream as if It Were Your Own

One of the most amazing qualities of dreams is their ability to be meaningful to someone other than their dreamer. Through working with another person's dream, you can receive significant, highly personal insights about yourself.

EXERCISE 7

Draw a Dream and Tell the Story

Dreams are primarily pictures; new perceptions can emerge when they are rendered visually. First, your partner draws a picture of his or her dream. Then you create a "dream" about that drawing. This exercise can free some of your unconscious feelings to rise to the surface.

E X E R C I S E   8

Montague Ullman's Dream Group Exercise

Montague Ullman has devised a dream group exercise that helps the dreamer understand his dream while at the same time enabling the other group members to receive personal value from it.

E X E R C I S E   9

Free Association

This exercise, based on one of Freud's most acclaimed theoretical contributions, consists of writing your associations to each word of your account of your dream, and then rewriting the dream using just those associations. Your dream's message is thus revealed in a barrage of hard-hitting ideas and images.

E X E R C I S E   1 0

Amplification

This Jungian exercise entails expanding and elaborating key dream images. When you explore an image in as much detail and in as many ways as you can, its true identity and meaning will emerge for you.

E X E R C I S E   1 1

Completing the Plot

The connection between dream life and waking life is a two-way street; this Jungian exercise uses that correlation to give you an enhanced sense of power in your waking life through creating a positive resolution to a problematical dream situation.

E X E R C I S E   1 2

Be Everything in Your Dream

Like Jung, Fritz Perls believed that you are every part of your dream. This gestalt exercise gives you the opportunity to experience all those aspects and thus get in touch with neglected or hidden facets of yourself.

E X E R C I S E   1 3

Fight to the End—From Victim to Victor

Dreams provide the ideal arena for confronting your worst fears. Conquering your dream enemies instead of retreating or capitulating can give you added strength and courage in coping with your waking fears.

E X E R C I S E   1 4

Demand Gifts from Your Dream Enemies

The Senoi aborigines were taught not just to defeat their
dream foes but also to demand gifts from them. This exercise can provide you with valuable "objects," experiences, and insights, and help you receive the maximum
potential benefits of your dream.

E X E R C I S E   1 5

Make Your Dream End Happily

This exercise, also based on the Senoi dream culture,
teaches you to move toward pleasure in your dreams, to
achieve your dream goals, and to create positive out-
comes for all your dream experiences.

E X E R C I S E   1 6

Make Your Dream Come True

Dreams can offer solutions to problems and fulfillment of
important wishes. This exercise can guide you in translating these benefits into waking-life experiences.

E X E R C I S E   1 7

Acting Out Your Dream in a Group

The Iroquois Indians regularly acted out their dreams. By recreating your dream with a dream group, you can gain new perspectives on both its message and yourself.

E X E R C I S E   1 8

Turn Your Dream into Pictures

Drawing is a direct route to the unconscious and can reveal aspects of an image that words alone cannot. Drawing your dream images can be a catalyst for otherwise unavailable associations.

E X E R C I S E   1 9

Incubation

You can make your dreams work for you by directing them to provide solutions to both creative and life problems. This exercise shows you how to instruct your unconscious to give you the answers and ideas you want.

E X E R C I S E   2 0

Self-Hypnosis

It's not necessary to wait until you're asleep to reap the creative and practical benefits of dreams. This simple relaxation exercise will enable you to establish that kind of connection between your conscious and unconscious minds whenever you desire.

E X E R C I S E   2 1

Stephen LaBerge's MILD Technique

The advantages of lucid dreaming are numerous and this exercise, originated by Stephen LaBerge, is an easy method of training yourself to do it.

E X E R C I S E   2 2

Look for Your Hands

Writer Carlos Castaneda was told that conscious dreaming was the path to power and was given this lucid dream exercise by the spiritual man, Don Juan. By training yourself to look for your hands during your dreams, you'll be able to trigger the awareness that you are dreaming.

E X E R C I S E   2 3

Push Your Dreams into Lucidity

By sharpening your awareness of prelucid moments in your dreams—those times during the dream when you suspect you might be dreaming—you can learn to transform an ordinary dream into a lucid one.

E X E R C I S E 2 4

Learn to Fly in Your Dream

Flying is one of the most exhilarating dream experiences. If you don't already fly in your dreams, this exercise can show you how to teach yourself to do it.

E X E R C I S E 2 5

Reenter Your Dream

Waking up from a nightmare only postpones the problem; it doesn't solve it. Reentering the dream gives you the chance to create a satisfactory resolution to the frightening situation.

E X E R C I S E 2 6

Become Friends with Your Foes

You can misinterpret a dream character's true intentions as easily as you can that of a real-life person. This exercise will enable you to assess more accurately your dream characters and to develop powerful dream friendships.

E X E R C I S E   2 7

Rewrite Your Dream from the Other Character's Point of View

In all forms of conflict, it's essential to know your opponent as well as possible. This is especially true in nightmares, where you may be battling parts of yourself. Retelling the dream from the other character's perspective puts you inside the character and thus can give you an entirely different understanding of the dream and its message.

E X E R C I S E   2 8

Have a Dialogue with the Major Emotion in Your Dream

One positive aspect of nightmares is their ability to keep you honest with yourself. If you try to ignore your inner guide, it will scare you in order to get your attention. You can determine the cause of your inner guide's concern by having a dialogue with the primary emotion in your dream.

The dreamwork exercises above attempt to point out new directions for using dreams to gain self-understanding and to enhance your life. But there's no need to stop there; you can also use these exercises directly on your waking life. Here is a final exercise.

E X E R C I S E 2 9

Turn Your Problems into Dreams

Dream exercises can help you to explore previously unknown or inaccessible aspects of waking-life difficulties, thus opening up new approaches to solving them. The nature of the problem will determine which exercises work best. You can either work on the problem directly or write it up as a "dream." This compulsive overeater used the amplification exercise to explore his obsession.

Overeating

Insatiable desire, endless like a hologram, overwhelms me, compels me. When it arises, nothing else matters or takes precedence.

It begins with anticipation: feeling the urge creep out of its hidden home in my mind and quickly fill my entire consciousness. I fantasize about the sensations of eating—the look, feel, taste of the food, the physical motions connected to it—over and over. My desire is so intense and acute that soon that's all that exists, that's all I am; all the rest of me is submerged.

I'm drawn, as if in a trance, to the kitchen. I tell myself I'm not going to binge; I'm just going to fix a small snack. I'm mesmerized as I stand before the open refrigerator. With the first bite it seems that all control is gone, though I know I really lost control the moment I decided to walk into the kitchen. I cannot stop eating, anything and everything in bizarre combinations. I don't bother to put the food on a plate; I grab it right from the packages and jars—a couple of pickles, a torn-off hunk of cheese, spoonfuls of ice cream from the carton, peanut butter scooped from the jar with my fingers. . . . Each bite heightens my hunger instead of satisfying it. The food itself is less important than the actions and sensations of eating; I consume it so fast I barely taste it. I feel like I'll die if I stop; I need to constantly eat the same way I must constantly breathe.

I stop only when the guilt and shame from the damage I've inflicted on myself is greater than my hunger. Then I loathe myself for what I've done.

This compulsion seems like a separate person who steps into my body and takes over. He's been with me since the moment I was conceived and is ageless. He's needy, panicked, and frantically searching for something; his power comes from a desperate desire to survive. He wants to be filled and satisfied with love, but all he knows is starvation and crumbs. He does everything he can to try to paste the crumbs together so that they form a piece of cake. It doesn't work and he realizes it, but crumbs are all he knows and they're better than nothing. He can't risk the familiar pain of starvation to attempt to get something he's never experienced, and yet at the same time he despairs because he knows his desperate scramble among the crumbs will prevent him from getting the piece of cake if it does exist. He's so consumed by trying to paste crumbs into his fantasy of a piece of cake that he doesn't see the crumbs for what they are. A crumb could be a piece of pie or a steak and he wouldn't notice because all he's looking for is cake. And he'll hold on like a bulldog to the one experience that comes closest to satisfying his need for pleasure—eating.

Through examining and expanding his problem of overeating, this man uncovered feelings he'd never acknowledged before. It was clear his compulsion had nothing to do with self-discipline or willpower; it was part of a deeply rooted pattern that governed his entire life. He recognized that he tried to make crumbs into a piece of cake in his personal relationships as well. These were painful but significant revelations; they clarified some of his confusion regarding the results of his life. He subsequently entered therapy to get help in understanding and overcoming this self-destructive pattern.

There are innumerable possible applications of dreamwork exercises in both our waking life and dream life; the more you explore them, the more you'll discover ways to use them. One thing is certain: stimulating your right brain and gaining access to the avenue between your unconscious and your conscious through dreamwork will enhance your potential for experiencing a full, rewarding life.

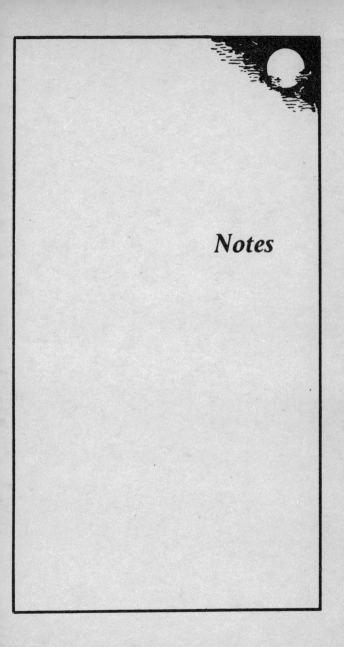

Notes

Introduction

1. Jones, Richard. *The New Psychology of Dreaming*. New York: Grune & Stratton, Inc., 1970, p. 27.

2. Quoted in Edel, Leon. *Stuff of Sleep and Dreams: Experiments in Literary Psychology*. New York: Harper & Row, 1982, p. 35.

1 The Science of Sleep and Dreams

1. Garfield, Patricia. *Creative Dreaming*. New York: Ballantine Books, 1974, p. 20.

2. Linde, Shirley Motter, and Savary, Louis M. *The Joy of Sleep*. New York: Harper & Row, 1974, p. 29.

3. Ullman, Montague, and Zimmerman, Nan. *Working with Dreams*. New York: Dell, 1979, pp. 34–35.

4. Jones, Richard. *The New Psychology of Dreaming*. New York: Grune & Stratton, Inc., 1970, p. 29.

5. Ibid., pp. 29–30.

6. Linde and Savary, p. 33.

7. Ullman and Zimmerman, p. 82.

8. Linde and Savary, p. 14.

9. Ullman and Zimmerman, p. 82.

10. Ibid.

11. Ibid., pp. 82–83.

12. Linde and Savary, p. 96.

13. Ibid., p. 21.

14. Jones, pp. 24–25.

15. Linde and Savary, p. 25.

16. Ullman and Zimmerman, p. 84.

17. Galvin, Ruth Mehrtens. "Control of Dreams May Be Possible for a Resolute Few." *Smithsonian*, August, 1982, p. 102.

18. Linde and Savary, p. 23.

19. Williams, Roger. "Twin Dreams." *Science Digest*, November, 1982, p. 26.

20. Ibid.

21. Jeffrey, Barbara. "Dream Breakthrough." *Women's Own*, June, 1977, pp. 35–37.

22. Linde and Savary, p. 85.

23. Ibid., p. 77.

24. Ibid., p. 85.

25. Jones, p. 66.

26. Ibid., p. 27.

27. Linde and Savary, p. 35.

28. Ibid.

29. Ibid., pp. 34–35.

30. Gliedman, John. "Scientists in Search of the Soul." *Science Digest*, July, 1982, p. 76.

31. Ornstein, Robert Evans. "The Rise of the Right-Headed People" (sound recording. Tape 20 from a *Psychology Today* interview). New York: Ziff-Davis, 1973.

32. Blackburn, T. R. "Sensuous-Intellectual Complementarity in Science." In R. Ornstein, ed. *The Nature of Human Consciousness*. New York: The Viking Press, 1974, p. 36. (Reprinted from *Science*, June 11, 1971, p. 172.)

33. Ornstein, Tape 20.

34. Blackburn, p. 36.

2 Diary of Discovery: The Dream Journal

1. Jones, Richard. *The New Psychology of Dreaming*. New York: Grune & Stratton, Inc., 1970, p. 46.

3 Images, Symbols, and Metaphors

1. Arieti, Silvano. *Creativity*. New York: Basic Books, Inc. Harper Colophon Books, 1976, pp. 44–45.
2. Fromm, Erich. *The Forgotten Language*. New York: Grove Press, Inc., 1951, pp. 19–20.

4 Dream Partners and Dream Groups

1. For more information on this exercise, see chapter 13.
2. "Dream Diagnosis: The Doctor Is In." *New Age Journal*, October, 1983, p. 44.
3. Ullman, Montague, and Zimmerman, Nan. *Working with Dreams*. New York: Dell, 1979, pp. 232–248. (In Ullman and Zimmerman, the six steps are included in their "Three Stages.")

5 The Legacy of Freud

1. Freud, Sigmund. *The Interpretation of Dreams*, trans. James Strachey. New York: Avon Books, 1972, p. 510.

6 Jung's Blueprint for Personal Growth

1. Jung, C. G. *Memories, Dreams, Reflections*, trans. Richard and Clara Winston. New York: Vintage Books, 1963, p. 159.
2. Jung, C. G. *Dreams* (translated by R. F. C. Hull). Princeton: Princeton University Press, Bollingen series, 1974, p. 101.
3. Jung, C. G. *Memories, Dreams, Reflections*, p. 133.
4. Jung, C. G. *Dreams*, p. 101.

5. Jung, C. G. *Spring*, ed. James Hillman. Dallas: Spring Publications, 1960.

7 Fritz Perls and Gestalt Therapy

1. Perls, Fritz. *Gestalt Therapy Verbatim*. New York: Bantam Books, 1959, p. 177.
2. Jung, C. G. *Dreams* (translated by R. F. C. Hull). Princeton: Princeton University Press, Bollingen series, 1974, p. 52.
3. Corriere, Richard; Karle, Werner; Woldenberg, Lee; and Hart, Joseph. *Dreaming and Waking: The Functional Approach to Dreams*, Culver City, Calif.: Peace Press, 1980, p. 78.
4. Ibid.
5. Perls, p. 74.

8 Discoveries from the Senoi

1. Noone, Richard, with Holman, Dennis. *In Search of the Dream People*. New York: Morrow, 1972, p. 32.
2. Corriere, Richard; Karle, Werner; Woldenberg, Lee; and Hart, Joseph. *Dreaming and Waking: The Functional Approach to Dreams*. Culver City, Calif.: Peace Press, 1980, p. 120.
3. Ibid., pp. 119–120.
4. Some recent researchers claim that the Senoi dream culture described by Stewart and Noone never existed in that form; they suggest that the anthropologists attributed to the Senoi a dream psychology and mastery they never possessed. This issue will undoubtedly be debated for years. However, there is no dispute over the effectiveness of the techniques themselves. See Faraday, Ann and Wren-Lewis, John. "The Selling of the Senoi." *Dream Network Bulletin*, March-April, 1984, pp. 1–3.
5. Corriere; Karle; Woldenberg; and Hart, pp. 112–113.

6. Garfield, Patricia. *Creative Dreaming*. New York: Ballantine Books, 1974, p. 89.

7. Ibid., pp. 83–84.

8. Called the Center for Functional Therapy.

9 Acting Out Your Dreams: The Iroquois Indians

1. Corriere, Richard; Karle, Werner; Woldenberg, Lee; and Hart, Joseph. *Dreaming and Waking: The Functional Approach to Dreams*. Culver City, Calif.: Peace Press, 1980, pp. 92–93.

2. Ibid., p. 98.

3. Fergusson, Marilyn, ed. "Teacher's Dream Comes True." *Leading Edge Bulletin*, November 8, 1982, p. 2. (*Brain/Mind Bulletin*, Interface Press, Box 4211, Los Angeles, California 90042.)

10 Draw Your Dream Images

1. Freud, Sigmund. *Introductory Lectures on Psycho-Analysis*. In James Strachey, ed., *Standard Edition of the Complete Psychological Works of Sigmund Freud* (vol. XV). London: Hogarth Press, 1963, p. 90.

2. Jung, C. G. "The Aims of Psychotherapy." *The Practice of Psychotherapy*. In Bollingen series (Vol. 20). New York: Pantheon, 1954, p. 47.

3. Morris, Jill. "Drawing in Modern Psychoanalysis to Facilitate Progressive Communication." Ph.D. dissertation, California Graduate Institute, 1981, unpublished.

4. Tavris, Carol (reporter); Visintainer, Madelon, Ph.D.; and Seligman, Martin, Ph.D. (researchers). "Mind Health." *Vogue*, May, 1983, p. 94.

11 The Creativity That Lies Hidden in Your Dreams

1. Quoted in Edel, Leon. *The Stuff of Sleep and Dreams: Experiments in Literary Psychology*. New York: Harper & Row, p. 205.

2. May, Rollo. *The Courage to Create*. New York: Bantam Books, 1976, p. 46.

12 Awake in a Dream: Lucid Dreaming

1. Faraday, Ann. *The Dream Game*. New York: Harper & Row, 1974, p. 341.

2. Galvin, Ruth Mehrtens. "Control of Dreams May Be Possible for a Resolute Few." *Smithsonian*, August, 1982, p. 104.

3. Corriere, Richard; Karle, Werner; Woldenberg, Lee; and Hart, Joseph. *Dreaming and Waking: The Functional Approach to Dreams*. Culver City, Calif.: Peace Press, 1980, p. 41.

4. Quoted in Colligan, Douglas. "Lucid Dreams." *Omni*, March, 1982, p. 70.

5. Ibid.

6. Ibid., p. 71.

7. Evan-Wentz, W. Y., ed. *Tibetan Yoga and Secret Doctrines*. London: Oxford University Press, 1981, p. 221.

8. Colligan, p. 70.

9. LaBerge, Stephen. "Awake in Your Dreams." *New Age Journal*, October, 1983, p. 42.

10. Quoted by Faraday, p. 26.

13 Decoding Your Nightmares

1. *Webster's Third New International Dictionary*. Springfield, Mass.: G.&C. Merriam Company, 1966, p. 1527.

2. Ibid., p. 1381.

3. Ibid.

4. Jones, Ernest. *On the Nightmare*. New York: Liveright, 1971, pp. 42–43.

5. Faraday, Ann. *The Dream Game*. New York: Harper & Row, 1974, p. 233.

6. Ullman, Montague, and Zimmerman, Nan. *Working with Dreams*. New York: Dell, 1979, p. 39.

7. Freedman, Alfred M.; Kaplan, Harold I.; and Sadock, Benjamin J. *Modern Synopsis of Comprehensive*

Textbook of Psychiatry II. Baltimore: The Williams & Wilkins Co., 1976, p. 71.

8. Freud, Sigmund. *The Interpretation of Dreams*. New York: Avon Books, 1972, p. 624.

9. Linde, Shirley Motter, and Savary, Louis M. *The Joy of Sleep*. New York: Harper & Row, 1974, p. 96.

10. "Dream Diagnosis: The Doctor Is In." *New Age Journal*, October, 1983, p. 44.

11. Siegal, Bernard, M.D., and Siegal, Barbara. "A Surgeon's Experience with Dreams and Spontaneous Drawings." *Dream Network Bulletin*, February, 1983, p. 1.

12. Quoted in "Dream Diagnosis: The Doctor Is In," p. 44.

13. Ibid.

14. Quoted in "The Meaning of Dreams. How to Crack the Code When You're in the Dark." *New Age Journal*, October, 1983, p. 50.

15. Perls, Fritz. *Gestalt Therapy Verbatim*. New York: Bantam Books, 1959, p. 61.

16. Edel, Leon. *The Stuff of Sleep and Dreams: Experiments in Literary Psychology*. New York: Harper & Row, 1982, pp. 302–303.

Index

ABOUT THE AUTHOR

Jill Morris, Ph.D is a psychoanalyst in private practice in New York City. Formerly a professional writer and painter, she approaches dreams from a creative and artistic perspective as well as a scientific, psychological one. This book grew out of a dream workshop Dr. Morris has taught at Cooper Union since 1982.